Teresa of Avila and the Rhetoric of Femininity

Teresa of Avila
and the Rhetoric of
Femininity

Alison Weber

BIP-90

PRINCETON UNIVERSITY PRESS

PRINCETON, NEW JERSEY

Library of Congress Cataloging-in-Publication Data

Weber, Alison, 1947–
Teresa of Avila and the rhetoric of femininity / Alison Weber.
p.   cm.
Includes bibliographical references.
1. Teresa, of Avila, Saint, 1515–1582—Rhetoric. 2. Femininity
(Psychology) I. Title.
BX4700.T4W45   1990   282'.092—dc20   89-39764

ISBN 0-691-06812-7

*To my mother, and
in memory of my father and brother*

_____

CONTENTS

ACKNOWLEDGMENTS

ONE DAY shortly after I had received word that the manuscript for this book had been accepted for publication, I overheard my two sons' musings from the back seat of the car. How long had their mother been working on this book? "She started it many, many, years ago," the elder said authoritatively to his younger brother, "when you were only a baby." They were silent a moment, in solemn contemplation of a project that has spanned nearly their lifetimes.

I confess this book has had a long gestation period. During these years (I will not divulge how many), I have been sustained by my family, friends, and colleagues. My sincere thanks are due, first of all, to those who read early chapters and encouraged my first tentative efforts at understanding Teresa's bewildering rhetoric: Antonio Carreño, Georgia Greene, Gustavo Pellón, Elias Rivers, and Charlotte Stern. Regina Harrison has been an inexhaustible source of wisdom, practical advice, and good humor.

Chapters II and III are revised and expanded versions of articles that appeared in the *Journal of Hispanic Philology*. I would like to thank the editor, Daniel Eisenberg, not only for permission to reprint material from these essays but also for his early support of my work, valuable bibliographic leads, and stimulating telephone conversations. I am also grateful for a grant from the College of Arts and Sciences at the University of Virginia that freed me from teaching responsibilities for a semester.

I am particularly indebted to my colleagues Javier Herrero and David Gies, who read the completed manuscript and shared their experience, insight, and erudition with me. From the day I arrived at the University of Virginia they have been unfailingly generous with their support and encouragement. As chairmen they have created in the

Department of Spanish, Italian, and Portuguese the ideal academic environment for the generation and exchange of ideas. For their guidance, their confidence in me, and their consummate collegiality I am most profoundly grateful. And to my husband, Michael, and my sons, Aaron and Joel, for their loving patience these "many, many years" my inexpressible thanks.

A NOTE ON EDITIONS AND TRANSLATIONS

ALL CITATIONS to Teresa's works in Spanish are from the 1962 edition of Efrén de la Madre de Dios and Otger Steggink, abbreviated as *Obras* 1962, unless otherwise noted.

I have used the translations of Kieran Kavanaugh and Otilio Rodríguez for *The Book of Her Life* and *The Interior Castle*. Elsewhere I have relied on the translations of E. Allison Peers. In order to highlight a particular stylistic feature or word choice I have occasionally substituted my own translations. I have indicated minor variations or clarifications of the published translations with brackets.

All translations for secondary works are my own, unless otherwise noted.

Teresa of Avila and the Rhetoric of Femininity

INTRODUCTION

ON AN OCTOBER evening in 1614 Spanish "galleons" and fiery "serpents" burst into flame in the skies above Madrid. Tolling church bells contributed to the din of the exploding fireworks as the entire city celebrated the beatification of Teresa de Jesús, the nun from Avila. Grandees, noblemen, ambassadors, and the king himself attended a mass in her honor. In the cathedral the nun's image was depicted with thousands of silk flowers: in one hand she held the palm leaf representing her virginity, in her other hand a golden pen that symbolized her eloquence. Poets vied with each other writing sonnets in a literary joust presided over by the popular playwright Lope de Vega. Similar celebrations with fireworks, bonfires, plays, bullfights, and processions continued for days in the towns where Teresa was revered as the saintly reformer of the Carmelite order.[1]

This jubilant outpouring of public veneration might at first appear to be a predictable reaction to papal recognition of a national religious figure. Amazingly, this first step toward Teresa's canonization took place only thirty-five years after she had been the object of examination by the Inquisition and only seventeen years after theologians had recommended that all her writings be burned. Teresa had lived constantly under the shadow of the Inquisition and had maintained beliefs for which some of her contemporaries had been persecuted. During her lifetime the papal nuncio had described her as a "restless gadabout, a

[1] These festivities are described in Fray Diego de San José, *Compendio de las solenes fiestas que en toda España se hicieron en la Beatificación de N. B. M. Teresa de Jesús Fundadora de la Reformación de Descalzos y Descalzas de N. S. de Carmen* (Madrid: Viuda de Alonso Martín, 1615). A copy of this rare book can be found in the library of the Hispanic Society of New York.

disobedient and contumacious woman, who invented wicked doctrines and called them devotion, . . . and taught others, against the commands of St. Paul, who had forbidden women to teach."[2]

How can we account for her survival, let alone her transformation in such a short period of time, from a controversial figure of questionable orthodoxy into a candidate for national sainthood? Charles Henry Lea, the noted historian of the Inquisition, remarked: "But for the accident that Philip II became interested in her, she would probably have come down to us as one of the *beatas revelanderas* [prophetic holy women] whom it was the special mission of the Inquisition to suppress."[3] More recent historians have also expressed the opinion that it was not the orthodoxy of Teresa's ideas but the force of her personality and her influence among powerful nobles that permitted her to survive.[4] Though Teresa's following in aristocratic circles was undoubtedly useful, noble or royal patronage alone would have been insufficient to save her had she failed to convince the theologians who examined her in person and through her writings.[5] By all historical ac-

---

[2] *Reforma de los Descalzos*, vol. 1, bk. 4, ch. 30, cited in *The Complete Works of Saint Teresa of Jesus*, trans. E. Allison Peers, 3 vols. (London: Sheed and Ward, 1944–1946), 3: 150, n. 2.

[3] Lea, *History of the Inquisition of Spain* (1906–1907; reprint ed., New York: American Scholar, 1966), 4: 17.

[4] Enrique Llamas-Martínez writes, "It was not her innocence which saved her. Fray Luis de León was also innocent and he spent several years in Inquisitorial jails" ("Teresa de Jesús y los alumbrados," in *Congreso internacional Teresiano 4–7 octubre, 1982*, ed. Teófanes Egido Martínez et al. [Salamanca: Universidad de Salamanca, 1983], 1: 137–167; quotation pp. 138–139). Teresa's noble supporters included Doña Luisa de la Cerda, daughter of the Duke of Medinaceli, the Marquise of Villena, the Duchess of Escalona, and Bishop Alvaro Hurtado de Mendoza, who was also a nobleman. She corresponded with the king, his confessor, secretaries, and advisors. Also see Arsenio Rey Tejerina, "Teresa de Jesús y su carnet de ortodoxia según su *Epistolario*," in *Santa Teresa y la literatura mística hispánica*, ed. Manuel Criado de Val et al. (Madrid: EDI-6, 1984), pp. 109–115.

[5] The visionary nun Magdalena de la Cruz was so highly venerated in

counts Teresa was a captivating individual who was able to win over even hardened adversaries with her great charm, humor, and humility. But her personal powers were matched by her persuasiveness in writing. In the uncertain theological climate of the late sixteenth century Teresa defended herself, as her earliest iconographers had envisioned, not only with the palm branch of her personal virtues but also with the golden pen of her rhetoric.

But did her writing reflect conscious rhetorical devices, or was it a sincere projection of her personality? Much traditional Teresian criticism has emphasized her antirhetorical, subjective spontaneity.[6] Teresa's writing does indeed impress one as spontaneous, since its syntax appears much closer to the oral than the written norm. There are sentence fragments, as well as frequent interjections, asides, and digressions. Lexically, there is also much to suggest oral language, such as diminutives, superlatives, and low-register, colloquial turns of phrase. Her spelling— *naide* for *nadie* and *milaglo* for *milagro*—implies a conformity to oral pronunciation rather than the written norms. We must consider as well Teresa's explicit disavowal of any literary pretensions: "habrá de ir como saliere, sin concierto" 'it must stand as it comes out, without harmony.'[7]

---

aristocratic circles that the daughters of important families joined her convent. When Philip II was born, her habit was brought to the Court, and the infant prince was wrapped in it "to protect him from the attacks of the devil" (Jesús Imirizaldu, ed., *Monjas y Beatas Embaucadoras* [Madrid: Editora Nacional, 1977], pp. 37–38). Nevertheless, between 1544 and 1546 she was arrested, tried, and imprisoned by the Inquisition for "diabolical possession." María de la Visitación, a Portuguese nun who had blessed the ships of the Invincible Armada at Philip's behest, met a similar fate at the hands of the Inquisition in 1588 (ibid., pp. 123–126).

[6] Juan Marichal, while rejecting the thesis of oral transcription, nonetheless insisted on the antirhetorical *sincerity* of Teresa's writing. See "Santa Teresa en el ensayismo hispánico," in *La voluntad de estilo*, by Juan Marichal (1957; reprint ed., Madrid: Revista de Occidente, 1971), pp. 89–98.

[7] *Camino de perfección* (Escorial codex), in *Obras completas*, edición manual, ed. Efrén de la Madre de Dios and Otger Steggink (Madrid: Católica,

She frequently protested that, because of her ill health and economic worries, she did not have time to revise or even reread what she had written. According to her followers, she wrote "as fast as a scribe," often in a trancelike state with "her face inflamed."[8] All of the above certainly support the celebrated phrase of Ramón Menéndez Pidal, "Teresa habla por escrito" 'Teresa speaks in writing.'[9]

But Teresa's writing is also paradoxically deliberate. She herself had advocated "plain speaking" for the nuns of her order:

> También mirar en la manera del hablar, que vaya con simplicidad y llaneza y relisión, que lleve más estilo de ermitaños y gente retirada que no ir tomando vocablos de novedades y melindres—creo los llaman—que se usan en el mundo, que siempre hay novedades. Préciense más de groseras que de curiosas en estos casos.
>
> (*Visita de descalzas*, p. 634)

> Let them also be careful in the way they speak. Let it be with simplicity, straightforwardness, and devotion. Let them use the style of hermits and people who have chosen a secluded life. They should not use the new-fangled words and affectations—I think that is what they call them—that are popular in worldly circles, where there are always new fashions. They should take more pride in being coarse than fastidious in these matters.
>
> (*Method for the Visitation of Convents*, my translation)

Menéndez Pidal accordingly believed that Teresa at times deliberately adopted a "hermit's style," and noting such "rustic" lexical items as "*ilesia*" and "*relisión*" for "*iglesia*"

1962), ch. 30, p. 239; my translation. All other Spanish citations to Teresa's works in this chapter follow this edition.

[8] *Procesos de beatificación y canonización de Santa Teresa de Jesús*, ed. Silverio de Santa Teresa, vols. 18–20 of Biblioteca mística carmelitana (Burgos: Tipografía de "El Monte Carmelo," 1934–1935), 20: xxxviii.

[9] Menéndez Pidal, "El estilo de Santa Teresa," in *La lengua de Cristóbal Colón y otros estudios sobre el siglo XVI*, 4th ed. (Madrid: Espasa Calpe, 1958), pp. 119–142; quotation p. 125.

and *"religión"* he argued, "In cases such as these, deviating from correct forms undoubtedly was more difficult for her than following them; it was an act of ascetic mortification."[10]

E. Allison Peers, Teresa's dedicated English translator, defended the paradigm of an essentially oral style and unconscious artistry but found himself caught up in paradoxes similar to Pidal's. Peers insisted that Teresa was rarely either consciously or unconsciously literary: her syntax was "less that of the professional writer than of the good talker," she had "few artifices" but "many habits not usually found in literature." Her sharp rhetorical questions were a "lifelike reproduction of the inflections of her voice." But when his analysis of "habits" turned up such rhetorical figures as alliteration, antithesis, catalogue, or etymological repetition, Peers dismissed them as basically nonliterary or inadvertent. For Peers style was an expression of sincerity: "In studying her style, therefore, we shall be studying herself, and it is that, above all, which makes the task worthwhile."[11]

Many critics, like Peers, have adhered to an adaptation of Montaigne's dictum: "the style is the [wo]man." The corollary assumption is that Teresa's style is derived from a gender-determined predisposition to certain linguistic characteristics. Spontaneity and colloquialness have thus been subsumed under the rubric of "feminine affectivity." A typical example is Rafael Lapesa's assertion that "Teresa uses the precise, loving diminutive to tinge her entire thought with the most delicious femininity."[12]

This tendency to define Teresa in terms of a feminine mystique almost constitutes a critical school in itself; attributions of feminine charm are standard fare in literary his-

[10] Ibid., p. 24.

[11] Peers, "Saint Teresa's Style: A Tentative Appraisal," in *Saint Teresa of Jesus and Other Essays and Addresses* (London: Faber and Faber, 1953), pp. 81–135; quotations pp. 103, 113, and 82.

[12] Lapesa, *Historia de la lengua española*, 9th ed. (Madrid: Gredos, 1984), p. 318.

tories. Rodolphe Hoornaert writes that "Teresa is a woman first of all in form, in her somewhat precipitous sentence structure which tries to say everything at once. . . . Nervous, with an extremely mobile and lively imagination, . . . her poor words succumb under the weight she makes them bear. . . . Teresa is also a woman in the very structure of her ideas. She bases her thinking less on abstraction than on the juxtaposition of concrete ideas."[13] And Dominique Deneuville frames her scholarly compilation of Teresa's references to the sexes with affirmations of Teresa's "coquetry," "feminine demands," "feminine shrewdness," "tact," "maternal instincts," and "woman's heart."[14]

The discovery of Teresa's Jewish ancestry in the 1940s led to an alternative approach to understanding her style. Teresa's paternal grandfather was a convert who, like many others, had reverted to Jewish practices. In 1485 the Tribunal of the Inquisition offered a pardon to all those who confessed their secret judaizing. That year Juan Sánchez de Cepeda, his wife, and his sons (including Alonso, who would be Teresa's father) were "reconciled" to the Church in an *auto da fe* that required them to process barefoot through the streets of Toledo wearing the infamous yellow *sambenitos*. Afterwards the *sambenitos*, inscribed with the disgraced families' names, were hung in the parish churches.[15]

But how was this crucial information, which had been obscured by Teresa's early hagiographers, to be interpreted? The historiography of Américo Castro had laid the

---

[13] Hoornaert, *Sainte Thérèse, écrivain, son milieu, ses facultés, son oeuvre* (Paris: Desclée de Brouwer, 1922), pp. 152–153.

[14] Deneuville, *Santa Teresa de Jesús y la mujer*, trans. Fernando Gutiérrez (Barcelona: Herder, 1966), pp. 45 and 135–146. In a similar vein see Mauricio Martín del Blanco, *Santa Teresa de Jesús: Mujer de ayer para el hombre de hoy* (Bilbao: Mensajero, 1975).

[15] Narciso Alonso Cortés, "Pleitos de los Cepedas," *Boletín de la Real Academia Española* 25 (1946): 85–110; Homero Serís, "Nueva genealogía de Santa Teresa," *Nueva revista de filología hispánica* 10 (1956): 365–384.

groundwork, showing sixteenth-century Spain to be a society obsessed with "purity of blood." The *conversos*, or Christian descendants of Sephardic Jews, even those who had taken religious orders, faced intense racial prejudice and blatant persecution by "Old Christians." Since any kind of intellectual pursuit was associated with the *converso* caste, might not the "ascetic" debasement in Teresa's style have been an attempt to align herself with the "Old Christian" peasant class? This was the thesis Felicidad Bernabéu proposed in 1963.

However, when Castro himself reedited an earlier essay on Teresa, he rejected Bernabéu's thesis and argued that Teresa's debased style was an expression of her alienation from the educated theologians rather than an imitation of illiterate peasants: "She uses rusticisms not out of affection for peasants, (insufferable because of their Old Christian presumptions), but rather in order not to conform to what was considered proper by the 'false authorities' who had created an anti-Christian social order."[16] Castro saw Teresa's racial caste as a crucial but unconscious determinant of her style—and her mysticism: alienated from a world of racial obsessions and patent injustice, *converso* mystics like Teresa, Saint John of Avila, and Saint John of the Cross found refuge in exploring their own individuality. By rejecting false worldly authority and affirming their intimacy with God, they thus compensated for their lack of a socially esteemed lineage.

In spite of his new insights into Teresa's precarious social position Castro continued to adhere to the theory of stylistic spontaneity and to see Teresa's mysticism and her style bound up with an innate feminine affectivity: "Teresa, a very feminine soul, transposed her desire into thought, and her thought always sweeps along with it,

[16] Castro, *Teresa la Santa y otros ensayos* (Madrid: Alfaguara, 1972), p. 81, n. 9; Felicidad Bernabéu Barrachina, "Aspectos vulgares del estilo teresiano y sus posibles razones," *Revista de espiritualidad* 22 (1963): 359–375. The popular classes were notoriously anti-Semitic, much more so than the aristocracy.

like a delightful gift, her emotion and fantasy."[17] Although he professed to offer an alternative to early Freudians, who had diagnosed Teresa as a hysteric, Castro merely bowdlerized the diagnosis, presenting Teresa's literary gifts as sublimations of a blocked—but nonerotic—female emotionalism.[18]

In a highly influential 1968 essay Francisco Márquez Villanueva gave a more complex picture of Teresa's "conflictive" historical circumstances, as both a *conversa* and a woman, without resorting to condescending sexual stereotypes. Márquez Villanueva was the first to suggest a consciously subversive element in Teresa's writing, necessitated by the prejudices against *conversos* and obstacles she faced as a women writing about mystical phenomena at a time when the Counter-Reformation Church viewed such phenomena with great suspicion.[19]

The idea of Teresa as a skilled writer who adapted her style to conflictive circumstances was developed extensively in a book by Víctor García de la Concha that appeared in 1978.[20] He conceded that Teresa was not always a careful writer but insisted that she was, nonetheless, a talented rhetorician. The colloquial quality of her writing, he argued, reflects not an actual spoken norm but rather the influence of contemporary oral sermons and the new "colloquialness" in written language advocated by humanists like Juan de Valdés. Using the term *rhetoric* both in the traditional sense of a codified system of tropes and also as a strategy of persuasion, de la Concha emphasized

[17] Castro, *Teresa la Santa*, pp. 65–66.

[18] Paul Julian Smith observes: "The way in which male critics can both denigrate and idealize female writing is very evident [in Castro's critique]." See "Writing Women in Golden Age Spain: Saint Teresa and María de Zayas," *MLN* 102 (1987): 220–240; quotation p. 228.

[19] Márquez Villanueva, "Santa Teresa y el linaje," in *Espiritualidad y literatura en el siglo XVI* (Madrid: Alfaguara, 1968), pp. 141–205.

[20] de la Concha, *El arte literario de Santa Teresa* (Barcelona: Ariel, 1978). For a concise overview of criticism on Teresa's style see Emilio Orozco Díaz, *Expresión, comunicación y estilo en la obra de Santa Teresa* (Granada: Diputación provincial de Granada, 1987), pp. 29–47.

Teresa's considerable skill in adapting her style to her addressees, especially when they were uneducated women. Her desire to share her experiences with other nuns required her to develop a "poetics for women" that was precise and persuasive but that avoided a standard theological vocabulary or pedagogical terminology. De la Concha has written, with intentional ambiguity, of Teresa's "rhetoric *for* women," that is, her need to find a language appropriate for women writers and accessible to women readers. The title of my book reflects my debt to de la Concha's considerable achievement: most criticism after de la Concha has recognized that Teresa's style cannot be isolated from the pragmatics of writing as a woman in Counter-Reformation Spain.

When I first read Teresa's autobiography, I was struck by the profusion of self-depreciatory remarks—confessions of wretchedness and incompetence that seemed hyperbolic, even for the text of a canonized saint. I was forced to confront directly the paradox of rhetoric and sincerity. Did Teresa really believe she was "the most wretched person on earth," or was she simply utilizing long-standing humility topics? Or was self-depreciation the only self-referential language available for women? As I read more and understood more clearly the conditions under which Teresa wrote, I was convinced that Teresa's self-depreciation was rhetorical but that it had a very nontraditional function. It seemed possible that Teresa's "rhetoric for women" was a "rhetoric of femininity," that is, a strategy which exploited certain stereotypes about women's character and language. Rather than "writing like a woman," perhaps Teresa wrote as she believed women were *perceived* to speak.

In exploring this hypothesis I found intriguing parallels between my own questions and those posed by recent studies on language and gender in contemporary society. In the 1970s a number of sociolinguists attempted to challenge stereotypes about women's speech—for example, the notion that it is more emotional or less abstract than men's. Their goal was to describe sex *markers*, or verifiable syntactical, lexical, and phonological differences between men's and women's language.[21] However, the original "genderlect" model hypothesized a much greater degree of homogeneity in the language of each sex than turned out to be the case. Many of the specific features posited were not supported by subsequent empirical research. Gender alone appears to account for very few discrete differences in language use. Many observed differences were in fact the result of coincidental correlations between sex and other social variables, such as age, discourse role, socioeconomic status, and ethnicity.[22] As Penelope Brown and Stephen Levinson have stated:

> Except for some paralinguistic features and some rare instances of linguistic features categorically reserved for one sex or the other, the linguistic markers of sex derive from one of two sources. . . . Either they are markers indicating the hierarchical relationship between the sexes, and so only indirectly markers of sex *per se* (and directly markers of deference or power), or they stem from the different social networks or activities in which members of the two sexes are involved in some societies.[23]

Research in the "second decade" has consequently centered on discourse interaction that allows gender to be

[21] Robin Lakoff's enormously influential 1973 article "Language and Women's Place" posited a discrete "woman's language" (reprinted in *Language and Women's Place* [New York: Harper and Row, 1975]). Cheris Kramerae introduced the term "genderlect" in "Women's Speech: Separate But Unequal?" in *Language and Sex: Difference and Dominance*, ed. Barrie Thorne and Nancy Henley (Rowley, Mass.: Newbury House, 1975), pp. 43–56.

[22] Philip M. Smith, "Sex Markers in Speech," in *Social Markers in Speech*, ed. Klaus R. Scherer and Howard Giles (Cambridge: At the University Press, 1979), pp. 109–146.

[23] Brown and Levinson, "Social Structure, Group and Interaction," in *Social Markers in Speech*, ed. Klaus R. Sherer and Howard Giles (Cambridge: At the University Press, 1979), pp. 291–341; quotation p. 328.

studied as a codeterminate rather than a discrete variable.[24]

Thus, although it had set out to challenge the unreflective biological determinism of sex stereotypes, the genderlect model was deterministic in its own right. Some theorists argued that the dominance of male language had left women as a "muted" group, unable to express their vision of reality or doomed to distorting their perceptions by adopting a "foreign" male language.[25] Alternative theories have conceded much more autonomy to native speakers of a language. Howard Giles, for example, has proposed that people have considerable ability to accommodate their speech *styles* to different addressees, accentuating or minimizing their membership in a similar or contrasting social group. A shift toward the perceived speech style of the addressee is known as *attenuation*; a shift away from the receiver's style (emphasizing contrasting group membership) is called *accentuation*.[26] For example, a black teenager might shift his style toward standard American English when applying for a job with a middle-class white adult but use more black English features when speaking among

---

[24] See Barrie Thorne, "Opening a Second Decade of Research," in *Language, Gender and Society*, ed. Barrie Thorne, Cheris Kramerae, and Nancy Henly (Newbury, Mass.: Rowley, 1983), pp. 7–24.

[25] The "muted" group theory is articulated by Shirley Ardener, "Introduction," and Edwin Ardener, "The 'Problem' Revisited," in *Perceiving Women*, ed. Shirley Ardener (New York: Wiley Press, 1975), pp. vii–xxiii and 19–27. For a critique of the theory see Deborah Cameron, *Feminism and Linguistic Theory* (London: Macmillan, 1985), p. 108.

[26] Howard Giles and Peter Powesland, *Speech Style and Social Evaluation*, European Monographs in Social Psychology, no. 7 (London: Academic Press, 1975); Howard Giles, Richard Bourhis, and Donald Taylor, "Toward a Theory of Language in Ethnic Group Relations," in *Language, Ethnicity and Intergroup Relations*, ed. Howard Giles, European Monographs in Social Psychology, no. 13 (London: Academic Press, 1977); Howard Giles, Klaus Scherer, and Donald Taylor, "Speech Markers in Social Interaction," in *Social Markers in Speech*, ed. Klaus R. Sherer and Howard Giles (Cambridge: At the University Press, 1979), pp. 343–381. In this last article the authors use the term "level two speech markers" instead of "speech styles."

his peers. Similarly, a woman might be motivated, under varying conditions, to exaggerate or tone down features that mark her as a member of the social group "women."[27]

The social determinism of the genderlect model has also yielded to a study of speech *strategies*. The emphasis for this framework is on speakers as rational, goal-oriented beings, motivated by a desire for freedom of action yet constrained by the need to protect "face," their publicly presented self-image. Plans of action are devised in order to accommodate conflicts between individual autonomy and social obligations, strategies in which the social distance of the participants and their relative power in society are crucial factors. As Cheris Kramerae has written, "Women, like men, will act to seek personal gains. But since women do not have the same status or the same resources as men, women will often use different means in order to have an influence on their own and others' lives." The strategy model therefore proposes that gender differences in linguistic *behavior* are best studied "as indications of and responses to a differential distribution of power."[28]

Although based on the analysis of spoken rather than written language, the strategy model is well-suited for application to Teresa's writing. Teresa did not write for an invisible public; she wrote for specific men and women, most of whom she knew well. The solitary act of writing was inevitably an expression of social relationships, frequently ones with a problematical distribution of power. Similarly, the "speech styles" concept has proved to be a useful framework for studying Teresa's approach to male

[27] Kramerae discusses the possibility of extending the "speech styles" model to gender studies in *Women and Men Speaking* (Rowley, Mass.: Newbury House, 1981), pp. 90–108.

[28] Ibid., pp. 118–125 and 142–154; quotations pp. 120, 153. Kramerae, the most forceful proponent of the strategy model, acknowledges the contribution of anthropological linguists Penelope Brown and Stephen Levinson, "Universals in Language Usage: Politeness Phenomena," in *Questions and Politeness: Strategies in Social Interaction*, ed. Esther Goody (Cambridge: At the University Press, 1978).

versus female readers and for analyzing the recurrence of such "feminine" features as diminutives, self-depreciation, and self-irony. This model has therefore led me to propose that what some of Teresa's admirers have described as her irrepressible feminine "charm" or "coquetry" might be better understood as covert strategies of empowerment.

My approach, therefore, has been to foreground gender as a stylistic determinant, without denying its correlation with other social variables. Teresa's style is seen as a pattern of linguistic choice motivated by deliberate strategies and constrained by social roles. I have found that by exploiting features from the low-register, private discourse of subordinate groups in general, and women in particular, she created a discourse that was at once public and private, didactic and affiliative, authoritative and familiar.

Strategy may imply to some readers not so much a "plan of action" as a conscious manipulation of others. I do not wish to suggest the image of a Machiavellian Teresa but rather someone closer to an Aristotelian *eiron*. In the *Ethics* Aristotle places the *alazon* or hypocrite on one side of the truth-telling mean and on the opposite side the *eiron* or character who disavows all admirable qualities. If, like the hypocrite, the *eiron* intends to deceive his audience, he does so "not for gain but to avoid parade."[29] This is an extraordinarily apt description of Teresa. In Chapter I, I describe the historical circumstances that made it imperative for Teresa to "avoid parade" by affirming her membership in the social group of *"mujercillas"*—or "little women." Chapters II through IV concentrate on specific manifestations of this strategy—humility, irony, obfuscation—in the context of individual works.

Although much of this book is devoted to explaining Teresa's deliberate strategy, I have also been led to speculate on why Teresa wrote so prodigiously and so obses-

[29] *The Nicomachean Ethics*, trans. David Ross (London: Oxford University Press, 1925), pp. 1127b, 31–32.

sively. It is not necessary to be a Freudian to recognize that unacknowledged motives may be concealed behind our conscious goals; that we betray unresolved conflicts when we speak or write; that the resolution we seek in the written word may be incomplete. I argue in Chapter II that the command to defend herself placed Teresa in a double bind because it was impossible for her to obey authority without challenging it. But the conflict between obedience to authority and authenticity played out on the larger social stage can also be seen as a reification of conflicts in a more intimate sphere—the double bind of the adolescent passage. Chapter V returns to the concept of the double bind; *The Book of Foundations* bespeaks Teresa's "unfinished business," her continuing struggle to reconcile her love for and resistance to authority.

Paul Hernadi has proposed, with elegant simplicity, three axioms of critical understanding: "Writers communicate, texts conceal, and readings disclose."[30] I hope that by disclosing Teresa's rhetoric we can better understand not only the story Teresa wanted to communicate but the story her texts conceal. Her rhetoric of femininity was self-conscious, alternatively defensive and affiliative, and above all subversive; it allowed her to break the Pauline silence. But her success also led to a self-subversion, for through her insistent writing she found the means to silence voices she did not want to hear.

---

[30] Hernadi, "Criticism as Re-presentation, Evaluation and Communication," in *What is Criticism?* ed. Paul Hernadi (Bloomington: Indiana University Press, 1981), pp. ix–xvi; quotation p. xiv.

Chapter I

LITTLE WOMEN: COUNTER-REFORMATION MISOGYNY

"A VIRILE WOMAN," "a manly soul," "She endured all conflicts with manly courage."[1] These are some of the most reiterated encomiastic expressions to appear in the documents related to Teresa's beatification and canonization. Teresa as a "virile woman" was the central conceit in many of the poems produced for contests in her honor: "You well deserve this name, because your deeds are not those of woman but of glorious man. . . . A Sage said (since it seemed impossible) that to find a strong woman, one must search to the ends of the world. Therefore it is appropriate that you were found among us, oh rare and divine miracle, since Spain was always thought to be at the end of the world."[2] When Teresa was proclaimed co-patron saint of Spain, a Carmelite friar declared in a celebratory sermon that she had succeeded in transcending the congenital inferiority of her sex altogether: "This woman ceased to be a woman, restoring herself to the vir-

[1] *Procesos de beatificación y canonización de Santa Teresa de Jesús,* ed. Silverio de Santa Teresa, vols. 18–20 of Biblioteca mística carmelitana (Burgos: Tipografía de "El Monte Carmelo," 1934–1935), 20: xiii, xxii, xlii. Many other examples could be cited.

[2] Diego de San José, *Compendio de las solenes fiestas que en toda España se hicieron en la Beatificación de N. B. M. Teresa de Jesús Fundadora de la Reformación de Descalzos y Descalzos de N. S. de Carmen* (Madrid: Viuda de Alonso Martín, 1615), 11v–12v. With almost identical phrases a Dominican preacher wrote: "If Solomon sought a strong, courageous and virtuous woman in his age, and could not find a single one, blessed is our age which has seen one of the most courageous and virile women that the Church has ever had" (cited in Félix G. Olmedo, "Santa Teresa de Jesús y los predicadores del siglo de oro," *Boletín de la Real Academia de la Historia* 84 [1924]: 165–175 and 280–295; quotation p. 170).

ile state to her greater glory than if she had been a man from the beginning, for she rectified nature's error with her virtue, transforming herself through virtue into the bone [i.e., Adam's rib] from which she sprang."[3] A 1614 text describes a hieroglyph depicting Teresa with walls in the middle of her body and towers growing out of her breasts. The accompanying Latin inscription reads: "Ego murus et ubera mea sicut turris" 'I am a wall and my breasts are like towers.' Saints Elijah and Elisha float above her on a cloud, proclaiming "Soror nostra parvula, ubera non habet" 'Our little sister does not have breasts.'[4]

It is understandable that a misogynist society would need to engage in this kind of linguistic (and pictorial) gender reassignment in order to designate a woman as virtuous. (The etymological correlation between virtue and masculinity needs no elaboration.) But it is remarkable that Teresa should have been the object of this transformation, since she had so often during her lifetime endured and embraced the derogatory epithet of *mujercilla* or "little woman."

WOMEN AND PAULINE SILENCE

Teresa was considered a *mujercilla* because, among other things, she "taught others, against the commands of St. Paul."[5] That is, she engaged in theological discourse at a

[3] Fray Francisco de Jesús, in *Relación sencilla y fiel de las Fiestas que el rey D. Felipe IIII nuestro Señor hizo* . . . (Facticio volume: Vatican Library, 1627), cited in Francis Cerdan, "Santa Teresa en *Los sermones del patronato* (1627)," in *Santa Teresa y la literatura mística hispánica*, ed. Manuel Criado de Val (Madrid: EDI–6, 1984), pp. 601–608; quotation p. 606. Also see Francisco López Estrada, "Cohetes para Teresa: La relación de 1627 sobre las Fiestas de Madrid par el Patronato de España de Santa Teresa de Jesús y la polémica sobre el mismo," in *Congreso internacional Teresiano 4–7 octubre, 1982*, ed. Teófanes Egido Martínez et al. (Salamanca: Universidad de Salamanca, 1983), 2: 637–681, esp. 654–655.

[4] Diego de San José, *Compendio*, 73r.

[5] This was the pronouncement of Papal Nuncio Felipe Sega. See Introduction, pp. 3–4.

time when this was a proscribed activity for women. Paul's justification for the exclusion of women from an apostolic role bears repeating: "Let your women keep silence in the churches: for it is not permitted unto them to speak; but they are commanded to be under obedience, as also saith the law. And if they will learn any thing, let them ask their husbands at home: for it is a shame for women to speak in the church" (1 Cor. 14:34–37). The position against women is even more restricted in the pastoral Epistles, written near the end of the first century A.D.: "Let the woman learn in silence with all subjection. But I suffer not a woman to teach, nor to usurp authority over the man, but to be in silence. For Adam was first formed, then Eve. And Adam was not deceived, but the woman being deceived was in the transgression" (1 Tim. 2:11–14).

The early Church fathers believed that women's intellectual inferiority and sensuality make them especially susceptible to deception by false prophets: "For [false prophets] are they which creep into houses, and lead captive silly women laden with sins, led away with divers lusts, ever learning, and never able to come to the knowledge of the truth" (2 Tim. 3:6–7).[6] John Gerson's (d. 1429) words are representative of a particularly rigid interpretation of these biblical passages:

> The female sex is forbidden on apostolic authority to teach in public, that is either by word or by writing. . . . All women's teaching, particularly formal teaching by word and writing, is to be held suspect unless it has been diligently examined, and much more fully than men's. The reason is clear: common law—and not any kind of common law, but that which comes from on high—forbids them. And why? Be-

---

[6] For the historical background on women in early Church history see Constance F. Parvey, "The Theology and Leadership of Women in the New Testament," in *Religion and Sexism*, ed. Rosemary Ruether (New York: Simon and Schuster, 1974), pp. 117–149. Parvey notes that the later pastoral Epistles reflect a heightened concern over the influence of Gnostic teachers and ecstatic sects among women (p. 136).

cause they are easily seduced and determined seducers; and because it is not proved that they are witnesses to divine grace.[7]

The belief in feminine spiritual inadequacy is perhaps best summarized in Kramer and Sprenger's 1486 handbook on witchcraft, *Malleus Malleficarum*. According to the fantastic etymology proposed by these authors, *femina* is derived from *fe minus*—lacking in faith.

Nevertheless, at various times in Church history women have been permitted to express their religious experience in writing. Thomistic theology, while essentially andro-centric, did concede the possibility of a prophetic role for women.[8] The explosion of female piety in the late medie-val Church is recorded in the visions of women mystics such as Julian of Norwich, Mechtild of Magdeburg, and Catherine of Siena. Such literature was not only a socially sanctioned activity for women;[9] as Caroline Bynum has ar-gued, women's visionary writings propagated new forms of late medieval Christian piety and created a religious lan-guage inspired by uniquely female experiences.[10]

MULIERCULAE AND THE PRE-REFORMATION

At the beginning of the sixteenth century Christian hu-manists began to reject explicitly the idea of the spiritual

[7] *De examinatione doctrinam*, pt. 1, cited in Edmund Colledge and James Walsh, eds., *Book of Showings* by Julian of Norwich, 2 vols. (Toronto: Pon-tifical Institute of Mediaeval Studies, 1978), 1: 151.

[8] Eleanor Commo McLaughlin, "Equality of Souls, Inequality of Sexes: Women in Medieval Theology," in *Religion and Sexism*, ed. Rosemary Ruether (New York: Simon and Schuster, 1974), pp. 213–266; quotation p. 236.

[9] "Visions were a socially sanctioned activity that freed a woman from conventional female roles by identifying her as a genuine religious figure. They brought her to the attention of others, giving her a public language she could use to teach and learn" (Elizabeth Petroff, *Medieval Women's Visionary Literature* [New York: Oxford, 1986], p. 6).

[10] Bynum, *Jesus as Mother: Studies in the Spirituality of the High Middle Ages* (Berkeley: University of California Press, 1982).

inferiority of women and to advocate expanded religious education for them. In the *Paraclesis* or *Exhortation to Diligent Study of Scripture* (1516), Erasmus exhorted all Christians—including women—to study the "philosophy of Christ," declaring that specialized learning was not necessary to approach the Scriptures: "But this delectable doctrine doth apply herself equally to all men submitting herself unto us while we are children tempering her tune after our capacity, feeding us with milk. She refuseth no age, no kind, [whether man or woman] no fortune no state and consideration."[11] Jesus did not want his teachings to remain secret but to be widespread, Erasmus argued. Accordingly, the Scriptures should be translated into the vernacular to make them accessible to all: "I would desire all women [*mulierculae*] should read the gospels and Paul's Espistles, and I would to God they were translated into the tongues of all men." Erasmus' defense of the rights of women to study the Scriptures is reflected in his vindication of the diminutive *mulierculae*: in the *Exhortation mulierculae* are not Pauline "silly women" but simple, unlettered women.

This movement of evangelical democratization, transcending gender and class barriers, flourished in early sixteenth-century Spain during the ascendancy of Cardinal Ximénez Cisneros. Under his tutelage portions of the Scriptures and numerous devotional and mystical works were translated into Spanish and distributed to convents and monasteries. The accessibility of works of St. Catherine of Siena, Saint Claire, Saint Juana de Orvieto, Gerson, and St. John Climaco in the vernacular meant that many

[11] For Erasmus' Latin text I have used the edition by Werner Welzig in vol. 3 of *Ausgewahlte Schriften* (Darmstadt: Wissenschaftliche Buchgesellschaft, 1968). I have modernized the spelling of the anonymous English translation of 1529 (facsimile reprint, Amsterdam: Theatrum Orbis Terrarum, 1973). Dámaso Alonso has edited and reprinted the 1555 Spanish translation of *La Paráclesis o exhortación al estudio de las letras divinas* along with the *Enchiridion* (Madrid: Centro Superior de Investigaciones Científicas, 1971).

more women were inspired to participate in the wave of renewed evangelism. Furthermore, the cardinal, a former confessor to Queen Isabel, was an enthusiastic supporter of female piety. Many of his monastic reforms were directed specifically toward improving the religious life of nuns and women tertiaries. During the years of his ascendancy women were granted a greater role in the educational and administrative life of convents. He was, to the dismay of some of his biographers, a devotee and defender of women visionaries who flourished as a result of his reforms.

THE ALUMBRADAS AND THE BEGINNINGS OF REACTION

Although Cisneros had opened up the Church to women and laity, the later years of his reformation witnessed another religious phenomenon that was to have a profoundly negative impact on women's relationship to the Church in general and on the life of Teresa de Jesús in particular. Groups of men and women, laity and religious, began to meet in private homes to read and comment on the Scriptures. Although the groups did not share a unified doctrine, they held the common belief that the individual was capable of understanding the Scripture when inspired or "illumined" by the Holy Spirit. This is the assumed origin of the derogatory appellation *alumbrados* or Illuminists. There are two distinguishing sociological features of Spanish Illuminism. First of all, many of its adherents were *conversos*. The direct influence from Jewish theology is not at issue; rather, as neophyte Christians, subjected to ever increasing racial discrimination, they may have been especially attracted to a nonceremonial form of Christianity centered on a loving and forgiving God.[12] A second so-

---

[12] See Angela Selke, "El iluminismo de los conversos y la Inquisición. Cristianismo interior de los alumbrados: Resentimiento y sublimación," in *La Inquisición española: Nueva visión, nuevos horizontes* ed. Joaquín Pérez Villanueva (Madrid: Siglo veintiuno, 1980), pp. 617–636. For speculation on why *conversos* were attracted to heterodox movements also see Anto-

ciological anomaly is that women held major leadership roles in these circles. Isabel de la Cruz was recognized as the "true mother and teacher" of the Toledo *alumbrados;* María de Cazalla preached the Gospel to women in her home in Guadalajara; and Francisca Hernández exercised enormous influence over Franciscan preachers in Valladolid. It is difficult to determine why women should have played such dominant roles in Spanish Illuminism. We can only speculate that the translation of the Scriptures into the vernacular, together with the general receptivity of the Cisneros period to an anti-scholastic Christianity, afforded women domestic evangelical roles for which they could find precedent in the history of the primitive Church.

As Marcel Bataillon has shown, this movement of interior Christianity initially arose independently from Protestantism, although it sprang from common European roots of spiritual unrest. Later it easily incorporated analogous Erasmian ideas, which began to penetrate Spain with Erasmus' vernacular translations in the early 1520s. But a confluence of events—the death of Cisneros in 1517 and the beginnings of Luther's rebellion in the same year, the growing suspicion of Erasmian anticlericalism, and the intensification of anti-*converso* racism—moved the Inquisition to repress what it could only define as a native protestantism in the making.[13]

In 1525 the Inquisition published an edict against the *alumbrados,* an attempt at codification of their doctrine based on the trials of its main teachers. As far as can be deter-

---

nio Domínguez Ortiz, *Los Judeoconversos en España y América* (Madrid: Istmo, 1971), pp. 159–160.

[13] The best introduction to the spiritual history of sixteenth-century Spain is Marcel Bataillon's authoritative *Erasmo y España,* trans. Antonio Alatorre, 2d rev. ed. (1966; reprint ed., Mexico: Fondo de cultura económica, 1982). His thesis that Spanish Illuminism reveals common roots with but little direct influence from Lutheranism has not been seriously challenged since first formulated in 1937. Antonio Márquez, *Los alumbrados: Orígenes y filosofía, 1525–1559,* 2d rev. ed. (Madrid: Taurus, 1980), gives the best overview of the early *alumbrado* movement and reproduces the 1525 Edict and summaries of the trial of Alcaraz.

mined from the edict, the *alumbrados'* heresy was one of protestantism *sensu latu*: they denied the necessity of any sacramental intermediary between God and man and thus rejected the efficacy of external works as well as the authority of the Church to interpret Scripture.[14] What the doctrine of *dejamiento* meant to the *alumbrados* is still not entirely clear. The term appears to refer to a direct experience of God, achieved through a form of mental prayer that emptied the mind of thoughts. In the state of *dejamiento* the advanced adepts could surrender themselves to God's will, with the assurance that they would not be led into sin. The Inquisition considered two equally heretical implications: justification by faith alone and impeccability or the belief that once united with God a person could not sin. The 1525 Edict did not identify Illuminism as an orgiastic sect, but their supposed doctine of impeccability, together with the free association between men and women in small groups, were seen as dangers to public morality.[15] In short, the fear of Protestantism nourished by anti-Semitism transformed a tiny sect of evangelicals, in the Inquisition's eyes, into a threatening band of heretics. The prominence of women in such dangerous sects provided the

[14] Unlike Bataillon, who considered Illuminism to be a "movement" of interior Christianity akin to Erasmism, Antonio Márquez insists that the Toledo *alumbrados* constituted a native, heretical protestant sect, with justification *sola fe* and *sola scriptura* as basic doctrine (*Los alumbrados*, pp. 219–221).

[15] Isabel de la Cruz and Alcaraz were never accused of sexual impropriety. However, Francisca Hernández' relationships with her male cohorts were condemned as licentious. Charges of illicit erotic relationships between beatas and their confessors did figure prominently in Inquisitorial trials in Extremadura in the 1570s. The Inquisition considered this movement Illuminist, although there is no evidence of direct link between the Toledo Illuminists of the 1520s and this later manifestation, which was essentially thaumaturgical rather than evangelical. On the Extremadura Illuminists see Bernardino Llorca, *La Inquisición española y los alumbrados (1509–1667)* (Salamanca: Universidad Pontíficia, 1980), and Alvaro Huerga, *Historia de los alumbrados (1570–1630)*, Vol. 1, *Los alumbrados de Extremadura* (Madrid: Fundación universitaria española, 1978).

justification for reaffirming traditional ecclesiastical misogyny.

The Counter-Reformation's increased skepticism toward female spirituality and its eagerness to reinforce male hierarchical authority is broadly reflected in the decline in the percentage of female saints from 27.7 percent in the fifteenth century to 18.1 percent in the sixteenth.[16] However, the rapidity in the change of climate can also be appreciated by comparing the fates of women religious figures during the Cisneros period and its immediate aftermath. The enthusiastic sanction of a female ecstatic in the first decade of the century contrasts sharply with the persecution of the *alumbradas* only fourteen years later.

The life of María de Santo Domingo, the Beata or Holy Woman of Piedrahita, in many ways exemplifies the favored role of women ecstatics during the Cisneros period. Born of peasant stock in 1486, María never learned to read or write. Around 1507 she began to acquire a reputation for saintliness because of her mortifications, trances, and gift of prophecy. Although she was a tertiary or lay sister, she became so influential in the Dominican order that she was entrusted with reforming the convents and monasteries in the area around Toledo. Her raptures at court won her the support of the Duke of Alba, who endowed a convent for her. Cisneros was one of her devoted admirers— he even gave her a rope belt of St. Francis and solicited her prayers.

In 1508, at the height of her fame, the Pope sent his own envoys to investigate the authenticity of her reported visions and ecstasies. Fortunately she could count on the active support of Cardinal Cisneros, who considered her the embodiment of "living Christian doctrine."[17] After two

---

[16] Donald Weinstein and Rudolph Bell, *Saints and Society: The Two Worlds of Western Christendom, 1000–1700* (Chicago: University of Chicago Press, 1982), pp. 220–221, 225.

[17] Cited by Vicente Beltrán de Heredia, *Historia de la reforma de la provincia de España (1450–1550)* (Rome: Institutum Historicum FF. Praedicatorum, 1939), p. 82.

years of investigation the papal envoys not only declared her innocent of wrongdoing but also issued an edict proclaiming the miraculous nature of her raptures, visions, extended fasts, stigmata, and prophecies.[18] One of the marvels adduced in the 1510 Edict was María's ability to answer profound questions on theology and the Scriptures while she was in a trance: "Those who have seen and heard her agree that it is indeed marvelous that a poor ignorant woman [*mujercilla ignorante*] like Sor María, born and raised in a village should be able to answer such questions as well as and sometimes even better than any master of Theology or man of science."[19] One witness quoted the opinion of a professor of theology at the University of Valladolid: "He could not help but weep greatly upon hearing the marvelous answers that Sor María gave to his questions; and he told me, because we were very close, that he did not know why men bothered to learn anything other than to serve God, since that little woman [*mujercilla*], who had been instructed by the Holy Spirit, knew more than all the learned men of the Realm."[20] Here the diminutive *mujercilla* has the same positive connotation we saw in Erasmus' *Exhortation*: in the eyes of Cisneros and his followers a woman's humble ignorance was no obstacle to spiritual knowledge—ignorance could even give a woman the moral advantage.[21]

[18] For the history of Sor María, see ibid. and Llorca, *Inquisición*, pp. 37–64. He reproduces the edict in her defense in App. I, pp. 259–271.

[19] Llorca, *Inquisición*, p. 260.

[20] Beltrán de Heredia, *Historia de la reforma*, p. 107.

[21] After Cisneros' death María's activities were severely restricted. Although other political factors were undoubtedly involved in the controversy surrounding this woman, her "vindication" in the 1510 Proceedings indicates the extent to which Cisneros was willing to expand and defend the apostolic role granted to women. For further evidence of Cisneros' support of women visionaries see Ronald E. Surtz, "La madre Juana de la Cruz (1481–1534) y la cuestión de la autoridad religiosa femenina," *Nueva revista de filología hispánica* 33 (1984): 483–491. William A. Christian, Jr., notes that after Cisneros' death in 1517 the Inquisiton and the papacy began to examine cases of lay visionaries much more rig-

This willingness to concede interpretive and even vatic powers to an unlettered woman would be inconceivable just fourteen years later. In the 1524 trials against the Toledo *alumbrados* the Inquisition pronounced such apostolic activity by women *"atrevimieto"*—an act of effrontery. The woman leader of this group, Isabel de la Cruz, was accused of numerous breaches of magisterial authority: she read and taught the Scriptures "according to her own opinion" and encouraged others to do likewise with "simplicity of spirit"; she was said to believe that learned men were incapable of surrendering their will to the love of God.[22] According to several witnesses, "She wanted to teach and not be taught, and she contradicted what learned men said."[23] Her disciple, Alcaraz, gave her more authority to interpret the Bible "than Saint Peter and all the other saints."[24] Her role as principal teacher of the sect earned her the epithet of "mujercilla ignorante y soberbia" 'ignorant, proud, little woman.'[25] After five years of imprisonment she was induced to confess "that she lacked humility since she was certain that she could not be deceived and hence came all her effrontery in speaking of the Holy Scripture and teaching it to others, . . . and she confesses that she was in error in committing this act of effrontery, since she was an unlearned woman."[26] In a 1529 *auto da fe* Isabel and Alcaraz, their property confiscated, were sentenced to public penance, lashes, and life imprisonment.

The language used to describe feminine theological pre-

---

orously (*Apparitions in Late Medieval and Renaissance Spain* [Princeton, N.J.: Princeton University Press, 1981], pp. 150–151).

[22] Márquez, *Los alumbrados*, pp. 261, 262, 164.

[23] Ibid., pp. 280–281.

[24] Ibid., p. 101.

[25] Ibid.

[26] J. E. Longhurst, "La Beata Isabel de la Cruz ante la Inquisición, 1524–1529," *Cuadernos de historia de España* 25–26 (1957): 279–303, quotation p. 285. Also see J. C. Nieto, "The Heretical Alumbrados Dexados: Isabel de la Cruz and Pedro Ruiz de Alcaraz," *Revue de littérature comparée* 52 (1978): 293–313.

sumption is even stronger in the trial records of María de Cazalla, a *conversa* and follower of Erasmus, who was denounced to the Inquisition in 1532. One anonymous witness after another testified that she had gone to María's house and heard her read the Epistles in Spanish and that María, while "in the kitchen," had tried to teach things about God "in a way which was not good for women to talk."[27] In the opinion of one prosecutor, "This prisoner holds many arrogant, fatuous, scandalous and suspect propositions, assuming the office of preacher and teacher of doctrine which is conceded only to wise men who have taken Holy orders."[28] The proceedings include such accusations as

> Said María de Cazalla, teacher and dogmatizer of said *alumbrados*, preached to them in public and indoctrinated them, quoting for this purpose sacred authorities and psalms from the Holy Scriptures and declaring this to them in the vernacular, twisting the meaning of the Holy Scriptures and its doctors to her own evil and harmful end, and many persons went to hear her and they listened to her as a preacher, which was scandalous for the people, since she cannot and should not preach, being a woman, and even if she were a man, it would be contrary to apostolic right and precept.

Although she acknowledged she was guilty of presumption for speaking about doctrine, she denied that she intended to teach or held heretical doctrine.[29] After two years of imprisonment she was tortured but made no further confessions. Her sentence was moderate for one accused of heresy—a fine of one hundred gold ducats and public penance in the parish church.[30]

[27] Milagros Ortega-Costa, ed., *Proceso de la Inquisición contra María de Cazalla* (Madrid: Fundación universitaria española, 1978), pp. 259–260.

[28] Ibid., p. 32.

[29] Ibid., pp. 100, 132.

[30] As Bataillon makes clear, María was persecuted for her admitted Erasmian beliefs, redefined by the Inquisition as Lutheranism, at a time when Erasmus' thought had not yet been officially condemned by the

THE CONSOLIDATION OF COUNTER-REFORMATION MISOGYNY

In opposition to the charismatic evangelical freedom championed by Cisneros, and enthusiastically embraced by the *alumbrados*, the Inquisition was moving, in essence, to consolidate the power of a hierarchical mystery religion hermetically controlled by priests. In order to do so it was necessary to ensure that sacred texts were inaccessible to the laity in general but to women in particular, who were deemed to be mentally incapable of understanding the texts and inherently susceptible to diabolical influence. The struggle to regain control over the Scriptures and Christian doctrine, and the effort to exclude women from all but ceremonial forms of Christianity, is most dramatically illustrated by the trial of Carranza, Bishop of Toledo, and the censure of his *Commentaries on the Christian Catechism*.

Bartolomé Carranza de Mendoza at first would appear to have impeccable orthodox credentials. He was twice the Spanish representative at the Council of Trent in 1545 and 1551 and was a prelate favored by Philip II, having distinguished himself in his service during the Catholic Reformation in England. In 1558 Carranza published a Christian catechism in Antwerp that, in many respects, is a prototypical Counter-Reformation treatise. From his preface, "To the pious reader," we can see that his motivation was to produce a book of Christian doctrine that would correct the errors being disseminated by the Lutheran heresy. On the issue of scriptural translation, which had been left unresolved at Trent, his position is cautious: he acknowledges that before Luther the Scriptures were not prohibited in the vernacular. In fact, in Spain Bibles were

---

Church (*Erasmo*, pp. 209–211, 470–475). The reaction against women's charismatic leadership is reflected in Francisco de Osuna's 1527 work, *Third Spiritual Alphabet*, in which he warns his Franciscan brothers to consult the superiors for spiritual advice rather than "*mujercillas devotas*" who may be deceived (*Tercer abecedario espiritual*, ed. Melquíades Andrés [Madrid: Católica, 1972], p. 567).

translated at the order of the Catholic kings. But, he argues, this practice has become dangerous now that Lutherans have taught simple unlettered people to understand the Bible according to individual whim. In Spain the situation has become such that women are declaring the meaning of the Scriptures to men, against the commandment of Saint Paul. The Scriptures are like wine: they are not for the young and inexperienced, but they can be imbibed profitably if they are "watered down" with glosses and commentaries.

The compromise Carranza proposes is that parts of the Scriptures, those that contain advice, precepts, and examples of good behavior, can be read by everyone, men and women. Other parts of the New Testament that are relatively clear can be read provided the translations are not literal and are accompanied by marginal comments. The most obscure passages, like strong wine, must be kept from the laity. But there are some good and devout people, he adds, who are capable of reading even the most difficult portions of the Bible

> as well and better than those who know Latin and other languages. I don't say this because the sciences that God has communicated to men do not have their place in the Scriptures, but because the Holy Spirit has His disciples and illumines them [los alumbra] and gives them help. . . . I have experience of this and can certify that with my advice some people have read the Holy Scriptures and this has helped them live a better life. These included some women, for neither Paula nor Julia Eustoquium, noble Roman women at whose request Saint Jerome translated the Scriptures . . . were more worthy of reading them.

In future, more serene days, Carranza concludes hopefully, the Church will once again be able to distribute freely the "spiritual nourishment" of the Scripture.[31]

[31] Carranza, "Al pío letor [sic] de este libro," in *Comentarios sobre el Catechismo christiano*, ed. José I. Tellechea Idígoras (Madrid: Católica, 1972), pp. 109–115; quotation p. 115.

Carranza's moderate position of partial, guided access to the Scriptures for men as well as women was roundly attacked by a group of theologians who denounced the *Catechism* to the Inquisition immediately after its publication in 1558. In the following year Inquisitor General Fernando de Valdés not only placed it on the Index but also arrested Carranza, submitting him to imprisonment and a trial that would last nearly seventeen years. When a sentence was finally handed down in 1576, the *Catechism* was condemned, although Carranza himself was not judged a heretic.

The most conservative of the prosecuting theologians, Melchor Cano, found dozens of Illuminist and Lutheran heresies in the *Catechism*. What concerns us here in particular is Cano's articulation of the extreme position of Counter-Reformation misogyny. Cano was adamantly opposed to vernacular translations of the Bible, which he saw as the common denominator of the *alumbrados*, Erasmists, and Lutherans.[32] He repeatedly attacked Carranza for entrusting the Scriptures to women: the divine word is a man's issue, "like arms and money";[33] even if some women should read the Scriptures in Latin, they would inevitably misinterpret them;[34] encouraging women to read the Scriptures with their confessors "in corners" would only result in more Illuminist scandals. He also condemned Carranza's belief that laymen and women could aspire to interior spirituality, arguing that the *Catechism* only urged "ignorant and lazy little men and women" ('mugercillas y hombrecillos ignorantes e ociosos') to dis-

---

[32] *Censura de Carranza*, ed. José I. Tellechea Idígoras, vol. 33 of Archivo documental español (Madrid: Real Academia de la Historia, 1981). Annie Fremaux-Crouzet offers a perceptive analysis of Cano's misogyny in relation to his overall philosophy of political repression; see "L'antifeminisme comme theologie du pouvoir chez Melchor Cano," in *Hommage à Louise Bertrand (1921–1979): Etudes ibériques et latino-américaines* (Paris: Les Belles lettres, 1983), pp. 139–186.

[33] *Censura de Carranza*, p. 234.

[34] Ibid., p. 235.

dain oral prayer and the exterior ceremonies of the church,[35] distracted them from their labors, and promoted laziness.[36] Cano's elitist position, so antithetical to Carranza's image of the Scriptures as "spiritual nourishment," resounds ominously in the following categorical statement: "No matter how much women demand this fruit [the Scriptures] with insatiable appetite, it is necessary to forbid it to them, and apply a knife of fire so that the common people cannot get at it."[37] As one Jesuit remarked in a 1559 letter, "These are times when there are those who preach that women should stick to their distaff and rosary, and not worry about other forms of devotion."[38]

Teresa's lifetime spans this period of misogynist retrenchment, which is reflected in the semantic shift of the term *mujercilla*. In the Erasmian context the diminutive is not pejorative but descriptive: *mulierculae* are unlettered women—those who can read in the vernacular but not in Latin, and according to the *Exhortation*, any Christian, with or without Latin, can be a "theologian." In the first decades of sixteenth-century Spanish *mujercilla* was also used to connote unlettered women, as it does in the investigations of the Beata de Piedrahita and in the Spanish translation of the *Exhortation*. However, as the religious climate became more hostile toward women, it took on the decidedly pejorative connotation: "The literal, let alone the spiritual meaning of the Epistles, is difficult for wise men to understand. How much more so for the silly woman [*mujercilla*] who neglects her spinning and has the presumption to read Saint Paul. Holy angels, what a tempest! What business has a silly woman, however pious she may be, reading the Epistles of Saint Paul?"[39] Teresa was

[35] Ibid., p. 310.

[36] Ibid., p. 353–354.

[37] Ibid., p. 238.

[38] *Monumenta historica Societatis Iesu* 8 (Madrid, 1896), cited in Francisco Trinidad, "Lectura 'heterodoxa' de Santa Teresa," *Cuadernos del norte* 2 (1982), 2–8; quotation p. 4.

[39] Luis de Maluenda, *Excelencias de la fe* (Burgos, 1937), fol. 50, 1, cited

born when *mujercilla* could imply spiritual humility, "holy ignorance," evangelical poverty in spirit,[40] but during her adulthood the term came to connote any woman whose spiritual goals were too great, in short, presumptuous female spirituality that bordered on the heretical.[41]

TERESA IN THE SHADOW OF THE "ALUMBRADAS"

Teresa de Jesús was not an *alumbrada*, if we define Illuminism in terms that the Toledo group themselves would have accepted: she did not share their disdain for sacra-

---

in Melquíades Andrés, *La teología española en el siglo XVI*, 2 vols. (Madrid: Católica, 1977), 2: 558, n. 161.

[40] Although the disdain for human knowledge dates from the early years of the Church, Renaissance humanists had endowed such expressions as "holy ignorance" and "discrete ignorance" with new significance, reaffirming the universality of Christ's message. Without rejecting erudition, the humanist tradition stressed the need for knowledge to be accompanied by charity and love of God. See Aurora Egido, "Los prólogos Teresianos y la 'santa ignorancia,' " in *Congreso internacional Teresiano 4–7 octubre, 1982*, ed. Teófanes Egido Martínez et al. (Salamanca: Universidad de Salamancai, 1983), 2:581–607.

[41] The first appearance of the diminutive that I have been able to find in Spanish is from a ca. 1260 translation of the New Testament. The text is precisely the second epistle to Timothy which treats women's susceptibility to deception by false prophets: "ca daquestos son los que traspassan las casas e aduzen catiuas a las mugerciellas cargadas de pecados que son aduchas por muchos deseos." See Thomas Montgomery and Spurgeon Baldwin, eds., *El nuevo testamento según el manuscrito escurialense I–I–6* (Madrid: Anejos del Boletín de la Real Academia Española, 1970). The diminutive does not appear in Covarrubias' 1611 *Tesoro de la lengua castellana o Española* (Madrid: Turner, 1977). In the 1732 *Diccionario de autoridades* (Madrid: Gredos, 1963), *mugercilla* is defined as "a woman of little esteem; foolish. Regularly applied to one who has thrown herself into the world." In modern usage the connotation of sexual license has become more prominent: "A woman of little esteem, especially a prostitute" (Julio Casares y Sánchez, *Diccionario ideológico de la lengua española*, 2d ed. [Barcelona: Gustavo Gili, 1959]). Fremaux-Crouzet also observes that, among sixteenth-century theologians like Cano and Vergara, the diminutive *"mugercillas"* was a common expression of "irritated derision" applied to women with high spiritual aspirations ("L'antifeminisme," p. 150).

ments and exterior works, the veneration of saints, and the mortification of the flesh. She could never be said to have espoused their belief in justification by faith alone. But as a *conversa*, a woman, a reader of Scripture, and a practitioner of mental prayer, she was suspect on multiple grounds and associated inevitably with the Inquisition's ever-expanding definition of Illuminism. By the 1550s the Inquisition was beginning to perceive any form of interior Christianity as a screen for Protestant pietism or other forms of heterodoxy. Moderate theologians were willing to accept mental prayer, provided its practitioners did not reject the legitimacy of vocal prayer. But the opinions of theologians like Cano were in ascendancy: contemplative prayer should be limited to "learned men" with specialized theological training; it was not for women, be they religious or lay, and any opinion to the contrary had "the savor of Illuminist heresy." With the Index of 1559 all vernacular translations of the Scriptures and all vernacular guides to prayer and devotion were banned, including works by Luis de Granada, Saint Juan de Avila, and Saint Pedro de Alcántara.[42]

Teresa thus lived under the shadow of Illuminism and the ecclesiastical misogyny with which it was inextricably associated. Her writing must be understood as an attempt to differentiate her form of religious experience from charges of Illuminism, salvaging what she could of its affective mental prayer. Thus, she accepted the veneration of images but preferred to use them as an inspiration to mental prayer.[43] She repeatedly acknowledged her depen-

[42] For the debate on mental prayer see Daniel de Pablo Maroto, *Dinámica de la oración: Acercamiento del orante moderno a Santa Teresa de Jesús* (Madrid: Editorial de espiritualidad, 1973), and Joseph Pérez, "Cultura y sociedad en tiempos de Santa Teresa," in *Congreso internacional Teresiano 4–7 octubre, 1982*, ed. Teófanes Egido Martínez et al. (Salamanca: Universidad de Salamanca), 1:31–40.

[43] Juventino Caminero makes a number of interesting observations on Teresa's strategic antiheretical statements in "Contexto sociocultural en el sistema místico de Santa Teresa," *Letras de Deusto* 14, no. 30 (1984): 27–48.

dence on the guidance or correction of the educated clergy or *letrados*, while maintaining that those who had not practiced mental prayer were incapable of judging its orthodoxy. She accepted that contemplation was neither a necessary nor sufficient path to salvation yet urged her friends to pursue it in spite of all dangers. She did not deny the efficacy of vocal prayer, provided it was accompanied by the mental effort of sincere devotion. She avowed her obedience to hierarchical authority but placed the authority of her inner revelations above that of the Church. She acknowledged the necessary mediation of the Church and the merit of works yet professed that the divine union was ultimately gratuitous.

Stripped of their concessions and qualifications, any number of her beliefs could have been formulated by the Inquisition as heretical propositions. Teresa did in fact believe that true prayer is not words but meaning, that spiritual experience is superior to learning, and that God can be apprehended intimately. Historically the alliance between mysticism and Church has often been an uneasy one, for the mystic's ineffable, antiintellectual experience of the divine is, ultimately, nonhierarchical and antiinstitutional. Nonetheless, Teresa moved between orthodoxy and heterodoxy, holding the explosive theological issues of her day in oxymoronic tension, and came perilously close to losing all. *The Book of Her Life* was in Inquisitorial hands for thirteen years. In 1580 her confessor ordered her to burn her meditations on *The Song of Songs*, and in 1589, seven years after her death, theologians for the Inquisition urged that all her books be burned.

Teresa as "Mujercilla"

That Teresa was, of course, eventually successful in claiming her right to doctrinal discourse is manifested in the hundreds of editions and translations of her works, her canonization in 1622, and perhaps most significantly and most ironically in her election as Doctor of the Church in

1969.[44] But this success would have been impossible had Teresa not made some accommodations to the gender ideology of her audience. She has given us one of the earliest and best definitions of pragmatic stylistics: "Estamos en un mundo que es menester pensar lo que pueden pensar de nosotros, para que hayan efecto nuestras palabras"[45] 'We are living in a world in which we have to think of people's opinions of us if our words are to have any effect.'[46] And Teresa knew that this "opinion"—her identification as *mujercilla*—constrained the conditions of her discourse. After all, the famous theologian Bartolomé de Medina had denounced her as a "*mujercilla*," declaring that she and her nuns would be better off "in their convents praying and spinning."[47]

Teresa's defensive strategy was to embrace stereotypes of female ignorance, timidity, or physical weakness but disassociate herself from the double-edged myth of woman as seducible/seductive. In the following passage, for example, the diminutive *mujercitas*[48] is subtly ironic, as

[44] Teresa was the first woman to be accorded this honor, which was proposed by Pope Paul VI in 1967 in the aftermath of reforms of Vatican II. The Promoter General of the Faith wrote in the 1969 Decree: "The difficulties in conceding the title of Doctor to holy women which have customarily been adduced, based on Pauline texts and historical reasons arising from former heresies, have disappeared in our times. . . . Certainly, since the circumstances of our times have changed, not only in civil life, but in the very life of the Church, it seems opportune to concede the title of Doctor also to certain saintly women who have excelled in the eminence of their divine wisdom" (*Santa Teresa de Jesús, Doctora de la iglesia: Documentos oficiales del Proceso Canónico* [Madrid: Editorial de espiritualidad, 1970], p. 254).

[45] *Libro de las fundaciones*, in *Obras completas*, edición manual, ed. Efrén de la Madre de Dios and Otger Steggink (Madrid: Católica, 1962), ch. 8, p. 520. All other Spanish citations to Teresa's works in this chapter follow this edition, hereafter abbreviated as *Obras 1962*.

[46] *The Book of Foundations*, in *The Complete Works of Saint Teresa of Jesus*, trans. E. Allison Peers, 3 vols. (London: Sheed and Ward, 1944–1946), 3: 43; hereafter abbreviated as Peers, *CW*.

[47] *Procesos*, 19: 349.

[48] In Teresa's idiolect the ending *-illo* is more strongly derogatory than *-ito*, which can simultaneously convey positive and negative affect. Note

she argues that "little" women may receive more spiritual favors from God precisely because they are weak, whereas learned men have less need of these divine consolations: "Para mujercitas como yo, flacas y con poca fortaleza, me parece a mí conviene, como Dios ahora lo hace, llevarme con regalos, porque pueda sufrir algunos travajos que ha querido Su Majestad tenga; mas para siervos de Dios, hombres de tomo, de letras, de entendimiento . . . cuando no la tuvieren [devoción], que no se fatiguen" (*Libro de la vida*, ch. 11, p. 49) 'In the case of a poor little woman like myself, weak and with hardly any fortitude, it seems to me fitting that God lead me with gifts, as He now does, so that I might be able to suffer some trials He has desired me to bear. But servants of God, men of prominence, learning, and high intelligence . . . when they don't have devotion, they shouldn't weary themselves.'[49] She concedes to feminine timidity to show that she respects and suffers from the male admonishments that she nonetheless disregards: "Contradición de buenos a una mujercilla ruin y flaca como yo y temerosa, . . . con haver yo pasado en la vida grandísimos travajos, es éste de los mayores" (*Vida*, ch. 28, p. 115) 'For the opposition of good men to a little woman, wretched, weak, and fearful like myself, . . . among the very severe trials I suffered in my life, this was one of the most severe' (K, 1: 188). She disavows her lead-

---

the combination of affectionate and depreciatory connotations in the following statement: "Pues comenzando a poblarse estos palomarcitos de la Virgen Nuestra Señora, comenzó la Divina Majestad a mostrar sus grandezas en estas mujercitas flacas, aunque fuertes en los deseos" (*Fundaciones*, ch. 4, p. 507) 'Now when these little dovecotes of the Virgin Our Lady [i.e., the reformed convents] began to be filled, His Divine Majesty began to show forth His greatness in these poor weak women, who none the less were strong in desire' (Peers, *CW*, 3: 17). For other examples of *mujercilla* see *Fundaciones*, ch. 2, p. 501, and ch. 15, p. 538; *Cartas*, p. 1061. *Mujercita* also occurs in *Vida*, ch. 36, p. 153, and *Fundaciones*, ch. 12, p. 530. (All examples can be found in *Obras* 1962.)

[49] *The Book of Her Life*, in *The Collected Works of St. Teresa of Avila*, trans. Kieran Kavanaugh and Otilio Rodríguez (Washington, D. C.: Institute of Carmelite Studies, 1976), 1: 84; hereafter abbreviated as K.

ership role in the Carmelite reform by acknowledging her incompetence, which necessitated God's intervention: "Si bien lo advertís, veréis que estas casas en parte no las han fundado hombres las más de ellas, sino la mano poderosa de Dios. . . . ¿De dónde pensáis que tuviera poder una mujercilla como yo para tan grandes obras, sujeta, sin solo un maravedí ni quien con nada me favoreciese?" (*Libro de las Fundaciones*, ch. 27, p. 576) 'If you examine the matter carefully, you will see that the majority of these houses [convents] have been founded not so much by men as by the mighty hand of God. . . . Where do you think a poor woman like myself, subject to others and without a farthing of her own or anyone to help her, found the means to perform such great works?' (Peers, *CW*, 3: 143).

With disarming modesty she concedes to women's intellectual inferiority in a way that frees her to explore a new theological vocabulary:

> Havré de aprovecharme de alguna comparación, aunque yo las quisiera escusar por ser mujer, y escrivir simplemente lo que me mandan; mas este lenguaje de espíritu es tan malo de declarar a los que no saben letras, como yo, que havré de buscar algún modo, y podrá ser las menos veces acierte a que venga bien la comparación; servirá de dar recreación a vuestra merced de ver tanta torpeza.   (*Vida*, ch. 11, p. 47)

> I shall have to make use of some comparison, for which I should like to apologize, since I am a woman and write simply what I am ordered to write. But this spiritual language is so difficult to use for anyone who like myself has not gone through studies, that I shall have to find some way of explaining myself, and it may be that most of the time I won't get the comparison right. Seeing so much stupidity will provide some amusement for your Reverence. (my translation)

Writing on the *Song of Songs*, she argues that because of women's intellectual inferiority they are more receptive to an effortless, though fragmentary, understanding of the Scriptures: "Mujeres no han menester más que para su entendimiento bastare; con esto las hará Dios merced. Cuando Su Majestad quisiere dárnoslo sin cuidado ni trabajo nuestro, lo hallaremos sabido" (*Meditaciones sobre los cantares*, ch. 1, p. 323) 'Women need no more than what their intelligence is capable of. If they have that, God will grant them His grace; and, when His Majesty is pleased to teach us anything, we shall find that we have learned it without any trouble or labour of our own' (Peers, *CW*, 2: 360). In *The Way of Perfection* she champions women's right to engage in contemplative prayer as a vital Counter-Reformation "work": "Pues todas hemos de procurar de ser predicadoras de obras, pues el Apóstol y nuestra inhabilidad nos quita que lo seamos en las palabras" (*Camino de perfección* [Valladolid Codex], ch. 15, p. 228) 'We women must all try to be preachers in our works, since the Apostle [Paul] and our own inability prevent us from being such with words' (my translation). When, objecting to her active participation in the Carmelite reform, her enemies cited Pauline Scripture against her, she answers: "[D]íjome [Dios]: 'Diles que no se sigan por sola una parte de la Escritura, que miren otras, y que si podrán por ventura atarme las manos' " (*Cuentas de conciencia*, no. 16, p. 444) 'The Lord said to me: "Tell them they shouldn't follow just one part of Scripture but that they should look at other parts, and ask them if they can by chance tie my hands" ' (K, 1: 328).[50]

In these passages (and in many others) Teresa concedes to women's weakness, timidity, powerlessness, and intellectual inferiority but uses the concessions ironically to defend, respectively, the legitimacy of her own spiritual favors, her disobedience of *letrados*, her administrative initiative, her right to "teach" in the Pauline sense, and

---

[50] As part of the reforms of the Council of Trent, nuns were required to observe strict enclosure. Teresa's extensive travels in her efforts to found sixteen new convents were seen by her opponents as a clear contravention of this imperative. Her detractors had apparently used Pauline admonitions that women's activities be confined to the home (Titus 2:5 and 1 Cor. 14:34).

her unmediated access to the Scriptures. In sum, Teresa's pejorative references to her sex—with or without the depreciatory diminutive—concede to Paul but allude to Matthew.

Not all of Teresa's pejorative references to her sex constitute pragmatic concessions. She also took pains to differentiate herself from *alumbradas*, continually consulting her confessors and other *letrados* over her visions precisely to reassure them that she was not involved in *"cosas de mujercillas"*—a clear allusion to Illuminist raptures (*Cuentas* no. 53, p. 455).[51] Though her faith in the divine nature of her own raptures remained firm, events later in life shook her confidence in women's stability. The life of asceticism, enclosure, and prolonged periods of mental prayer in the reformed Carmelite convents, a life that she had hoped would open the mystical path for more women, had led several nuns along another path, which Teresa was forced to recognize as illness. She began to acknowledge the difficulty of judging ecstasy from without and of distinguishing divine communication from the effects of poor diet, self-inflicted pain, and sensory deprivation. Whereas Teresa consistently resisted the opinion that such women were victims of diabolical possession, she reluctantly came to accept the notion that women's physical weakness (*flaqueza*) had unfortunate mental consequences.

Teresa did make one unequivocal apology for women in

[51] Writing of herself in third person, Teresa records that she felt more shame in confessing her divine favors than her sins because "le parecía que se reirían de ella y que eran cosas de mujercillas, que siempre las había aborrecido oír" (*Cuentas* no. 53, p. 455) 'it seemed to her that her confessors would laugh at her and attribute these favors to the foolish things of women [and she had always hated hearing about such things]' (K, 1: 350). Alfred Rodríguez and Darcy Donahue note that out of fifteen references to women in Teresa's autobiography, thirteen are pejorative. They propose that many of Teresa's prejudicial remarks about women are motivated by the desire to differentiate herself from *alumbradas*. See "Un ensayo de explicación razonada de las referencias de Santa Teresa a su propio sexo en *Vida*," in *Santa Teresa y la literature mística hispánica*, ed. Manuel Criado de Val (Madrid: EDI-6, 1984), pp. 309–313.

COUNTER-REFORMATION MISOGYNY 41

the introduction to *The Way of Perfection*: "[No] aborre-cistes, Señor de mi alma, cuando andávades por el mundo, las mujeres antes las favorecistes siempre con mucha piedad y hallastes en ellas tanto amor y más fe que en los hombres"[52] 'Lord of my soul, you did not hate women when You walked in the world; rather you favored them always with much pity and found in them as much love and more faith than in men' (my translation). This is Teresa's most radical and perhaps most unorthodox statement, for here she claims not simply women's spiritual equality with men but their *superior* capacity for faith and their *favored* status in God's compassionate eyes. Her spiritual life was dedicated to finding and knowing this God who did not hate but rather pitied women. It is not surprising that these words never reached their intended audience but lay obliterated beneath heavy cross-hatches, twice censored by her confessor and by her own hand, until deciphered by modern editors. For a *mujercilla* the alternative to concession was silence.

[52] *Camino de perfección*, transcripción del autógrafo de Valladolid, ed. Tomás de la Cruz, 2 vols. (Rome: Tipografia poliglotta vaticana, 1965), 2: 68*.

Chapter II

THE BOOK OF HER LIFE AND THE RHETORIC OF HUMILITY

IT IS SOMETIMES convenient to refer to Teresa's *Libro de la vida* or *The Book of Her Life* as an autobiography,[1] although the first lines of the Prologue should alert us immediately to the ambiguous appropriateness of this generic attribution: "Quisiera yo que, como me han mandado y dado larga licencia para que escriva el modo de oración y las mercedes que el Señor me ha hecho, me la dieran para que muy por menudo y con claridad dijera mis grandes pecados y ruin vida"[2] 'Since my confessors commanded me and gave me plenty of leeway to write about the favors and the kind of prayer the Lord has granted me, I wish they would also have allowed me to tell very clearly and minutely about my great sins and wretched life.'[3] The text

An earlier version of this chapter appeared as "The Paradoxes of Humility: Santa Teresa's *Libro de la vida* as Double Bind" in the *Journal of Hispanic Philology* 9 (1985): 211–230.

[1] Randolph Pope, while recognizing that only the first nine chapters are autobiographical in a conventional sense, considers *The Book of Her Life* an important landmark in the history of Hispanic autobiography: "Teresa . . . sees her personal history as a dramatic conflict in which certainty does not exist and precisely because of this, autobiography becomes meditation, examination, drama and model" (*La autobiografía española hasta Torres Villarroel*, Hispanistische Studien, Band 1 [Frankfurt: Lang, 1974], pp. 46–71; quotation p. 71).

[2] *Libro de la vida*, in *Obras completas*, edición manual, ed. Efrén de la Madre de Dios and Otger Steggink (Madrid: Católica, 1962), Prólogo, p. 16. All other Spanish citations to Teresa's work in this chapter follow this edition, hereafter abbreviated as *Obras* 1962.

[3] *The Book of Her Life*, in *The Collected Works of St. Teresa of Avila*, trans. Kieran Kavanaugh and Otilio Rodríguez (Washington, D.C.: Institute of Carmelite Studies, 1976), 1: 32; hereafter abbreviated as K.

is clearly nonautobiographical in the sense that Teresa lacks a modern autobiographical motive—the desire to have others observe her uniqueness as an individual; hers is a document produced in response to an order from her confessors to describe her suspect practice of mental prayer and defend the authenticity of the spiritual favors received through it. But although the confessors' command to write marks her text as a religious/legal confession, the "leeway" they concede her allows Teresa to expand a written confession into a psychological as well as a theological *apologia*.[4]

Teresa's relationship to the men who ordered her to write the story of her life is complex. The confessors were not uniformly hostile adversaries; some were, or became "liberals" on the issue of mental prayer.[5] Nonetheless,

[4] In the context of Santa Teresa's period it is difficult to separate the ecclesiastical from the judicial. As Antonio Gómez-Moriana has noted, frequently a general confession written at the order of a confessor also served as a preliminary statement by the accused in Inquisitorial trials. Such documents were also used to effect pretrial reconciliations during a grace period conceded by the Inquisition ("Autobiografía y discurso ritual: Problemática de la confesión autobiográfica destinada al tribunal inquisitorial," in *Actes du IIe Colloque International de la Baume-les Aix, 23–24–25 mai 1981* [Aix-en-Provence: Université de Provence, 1982], pp. 69–94; quotation p. 72; reprinted in *Imprévue* 1 [1983]: 107–129). Francisco Márquez Villanueva was the first critic to point out the dual status of *Vida* as confession and apologia in "Santa Teresa y el linaje," in *Espiritualidad y literatura en el siglo XVI* (Madrid: Alfaguara, 1968), pp. 141–205; quotation p. 187. Also see Sol Villacèque's provocative analysis of the Prologue in "Rhetorique et pragmatique: La transformation du code dans le *Libro de la vida* de Thérèse D'Avila," *Imprévue* 2 (1985): 7–27.

[5] The first written confessions were prepared for Francisco de Salcedo, a layman who had practiced mental prayer, and an ascetic priest, Gaspar Daza. Both were inclined to believe that Teresa's experiences were diabolical. Baltasar Alvarez, Teresa's Jesuit confessor for several years, eventually became convinced of the authenticity of Teresa's favors. Teresa introduced two later confessors, García de Toledo and Pedro Ibáñez, to the practice of mental prayer, and both became enthusiastic supporters (K, "Introduction," 1: 16–17). Domingo Báñez, who wrote the official Approbation for the work in 1575, was of the opinion that "this woman, . . . although she may be deceived in some respects, at least is not deceptive"

given the Inquisition's persecution of Illuminists, they were understandably alarmed at Teresa's experiences and realized that they needed to protect her as well as themselves against charges of heresy. As we have seen, the post-Cisneros period witnessed a backlash against the type of feminine spirituality that had been promoted by the cardinal. In 1537 a Franciscan lamented, "For the last fifty years in this kingdom, how many people have been deceived—wise men, priests, monks, lords and ladies—by the fame of holy miracle-working females!"[6] And in 1546 the Inquisition instigated an investigation of Magdalena de la Cruz, a nun who was widely venerated for her fasts, vigils, prophecies, and stigmata. The Inquisition found that, in the words of a contemporary observer, "The devil had kept her as his lover [manceba] from the time she was six years old. At first she must have innocently believed that he was an angel of light; afterwards, she must have understood who this lover was, but did not want to turn back; . . . perhaps she did not want to lose her widespread fame."[7] In spite of royal patronage Magdalena was condemned to perpetual silence and imprisonment in a convent outside of Cordoba.

Teresa lived, inevitably, under the shadow of Magdalena de la Cruz.[8] In Chapter 23 Teresa acknowledges that

---

(*Obras de Santa Teresa de Jesús*, ed. Silverio de Santa Teresa, Vols. 1–9 of Biblioteca mística carmelitana [Burgos: El Monte Carmelo, 1915–1924], 2: 212). Ciriaco Morón Arroyo writes on the intellectual background of Teresa's main advisors in " 'I Will Give You a Living Book': Spiritual Currents at Work at the Time of St. Teresa of Jesus," in *Centenary of St. Teresa*, ed. John Sullivan (Washington, D.C.: Institute of Carmelite Studies, 1984), pp. 95–112.

[6] *Excelencias de la fe* (Burgos 1537), cited by Melquíades Andrés, *La Teología española en el siglo XVI*, 2 vols. (Madrid: Católica, 1977), 2: 558.

[7] This letter of Luis de Zapata (1546) and other contemporary accounts of the case are collected in Jesús Imirizaldu, ed., *Monjas y Beatas Embaucadoras* (Madrid: Editora Nacional, 1977), pp. 30–62; quotation p. 34.

[8] In the hearings on her canonization it was noted that the specter of Magdalena de la Cruz followed her throughout her life. See *Procesos de beatificación y canonización de Santa Teresa de Jesús*, ed. Silverio de Santa Teresa, Vols. 18–20 of Biblioteca mística carmelitana (Burgos: Tipografía de "El Monte Carmelo," 1934–1935), 18: 11 and 43–44.

news of the "serious diabolical illusions and deceptions in women," which coincided with her first mystical experiences, had terrified her. In sum, the Inquisition was casting its net wider to include not only heretics like the *alumbradas* but orthodox "frauds" or *embaucadoras* like Magdalena de la Cruz. Diabolical seduction, seen as a sexual possession by the devil, was emerging as the Inquisition's preferred explanation for ecstatic trances and other extraordinary phenomena. Although the laity embraced reports of women's thaumaturgical powers with enthusiasm, the Inquisition was moving to reaffirm the traditional ecclesiastical association between women's power and women's fallen sexuality.

Thus, the cautious support of her primary addressees did not free Teresa to write spontaneously and ingenuously about her spiritual life. On the contrary, the requirement to explain and defend her spiritual favors placed her in a double bind. The term "double bind" has entered the popular vocabulary and frequently refers to being on "the horns of a dilemma" or to any difficult choice, but such usage ignores crucial concepts of the theory. The double bind is not a difficult choice but rather the illusion of choice within a relationship. The alternatives are illusory because they exist on different logical levels. For example, the command to "be independent" is paradoxical since spontaneous behavior cannot be ordered; compliance with the order on one level violates it on another level. Such paradoxical injunctions are called *binds* not only because of the logical dilemmas they produce but also because they occur within an intensely important relationship that is essential to the subject's self-definition. In classic double bind situations (the parent-child is prototypic) the subject has no recourse to clarification from outside the relationship. There is a prohibition against "leaving the field."[9]

[9] Since first presented in the 1956 paper "Toward a Theory of Schizophrenia" by Gregory Bateson and others, the theory of the double bind has been the subject of extensive comment, debate and amplification. Today its significance is recognized to be as a paradigm in behavior and semiotic logic rather than as an etiology for schizophrenia. The original

The binding "field" from which Teresa wrote was constituted by ties that were emotional, theological, and legalistic. Her addressees were, after all, the very men who controlled her access to confession and absolution. Furthermore, as a woman without "letters" (or theological studies in Latin) Teresa could not presume to have the necessary theological learning to support her claims or fully understand her experience. Even if she could convince her confessors that the favors were not diabolical delusions, how could she do so without appropriating the male prerogative in theological disquisition? What special virtues had allowed her to achieve the mystical state of quietude while learned and pious men had not? How could she comply with the order to reveal her favors but avoid accusations of demagoguery? In short, to prove worthiness and humility at the same time implies the logical contradiction of the double bind, since humility is tainted by self-regard. As the religious writers of the times acknowledged, humility is a silent virtue, incompatible with self-defense. Fray Luis de Granada advised his readers: "Rejoice at being reprimanded and instructed by others, and if someone reprimands you in anger, do not defend yourself with pride, but desire to suffer more and be silent in imitation of our Lord."[10] More colorfully, Alonso de Madrid wrote, "Let us jump for joy a thousand times when we are insulted and slandered."[11]

---

paper is reprinted in Bateson, *Steps to an Ecology of Mind* (New York: Random House, 1972), pp. 201–227. A collection of significant essays and reviews of the theory can be found in the volume edited by Carlos Sluzki and Donald Ransom, *Double Bind: The Foundation of the Communicational Approach to the Family* (New York: Grune and Strathon, 1976). Also see the review article by David Olson, "Empirically Unbinding the Double Bind: Review of Research and Conceptual Reformulations," *Family Process* 11 (1972), 69–94.

[10] *Memorial de la vida cristiana* (1565), in *Obras del V. P. M. Fray Luis de Granada*, ed. José Joaquín Mora, vol. 8 of *Biblioteca de autores españoles* (Madrid: Rivadeneyra, 1884), 2: 282.

[11] Alonso de Madrid, *Arte para servir a Dios* (1521), vol. 1 of *Místicos franciscanos* (Madrid: Católica, 1948), p. 132.

In addition to the traditional Christian exigence for self-abnegation, humility was a virtue of special importance for the practitioners of mental prayer. Francisco de Osuna in his treatise on prayer, *Third Spiritual Alphabet* (1527), dedicates a chapter to the discussion of humility, which he considers the "sovereign virtue": "Know that this virtue [humility] assures the heart and explains the doubts that usually acompany the prayer of recollection, where sometimes one experiences such wondrous things from God, . . . that the soul wonders if all this is from God or if the angel of Satan has transformed himself in order to deceive the soul and make it fall from pride. . . . If you are humble, you will be on solid ground."[12] The Franciscans were, in short, determined to keep their spiritual practices free from all taint of demagoguery.

Humility is thus the touchstone of the spiritual graces received from the prayer of recollection—a virtue all the more necessary for women, who were considered more susceptible than men to delusions.[13] But paradoxically, this very Franciscan humility, as it provides assurance against self-doubts, intensifies the strictures of Teresa's paradoxical situation. Osuna further writes:

> Blessed is he who puts much effort in humbling himself by whatever means he can, belittling himself in his own eyes and in the eyes of all others. Do not wish for others to take notice of you, because this offends Humility, and Humility is very quiet and does not make noise of any sort; and although she sees that she has been offended, she does not complain, but only reproaches herself, because she felt the offense. When she is offended, she is silent, and only displays what is contemptible about herself, and tries to disavow her abilities and favors. (p. 551)

[12] *Melquíades Andrés, ed., Tercer Abecedario Espiritual* (Madrid: Católica, 1972), pp. 541–542.

[13] Báñez, in his 1575 Approbation of *Libro de la Vida*, expressed his concern about Teresa's revelations, which were to be feared "especially in women" (*Obras* 1962, p. 178).

Thus, although humility constitutes proof of the authenticity of Teresa's religious experience, it also requires that she silence what could be marshalled in her defense. This is Teresa's dilemma—to elaborate a rhetoric that can give a voice to a silent virtue.

Although the double bind was originally formulated as part of the etiology of schizogenic family structures, subsequent research has explored the salutary and creative responses to the bind. Double bind dilemmas can be handled without despair if the subject is able, in some way, to distinguish and acknowledge the interwoven components of the message. This may be done by giving a manifestly dual message in reply: instead of being paralyzed by the attempt to reconcile conflicting demands, the subject can reply illogically, with paradoxes of his or her own. A sufficiently resourceful subject can also break off or redefine the emotional dependency of the binding relationship. Finally, the subject can learn to metacommunicate—to appreciate and articulate the logical paradox in the bind, explicitly labeling its components.[14] I believe that one can find evidence of all of these strategies in the *Libro de la vida* as it documents Teresa's struggle to find a creative solution to the double bind.

"AFFECTED MODESTY"

The many references Teresa makes to her own "wretchedness" in *The Book of Her Life* have long perplexed her readers. For E. A. Peers,

> If there is one trait in St. Teresa's character which repels us it is a self-abasement carried to excess and suggestive of

[14] See John H. Weakland's article "The 'Double Bind' Hypothesis of Schizophrenia and Three-Party Interaction," in *Double Bind: The Foundation of the Communicational Approach to the Family*, ed. Carlos Sluzki and Donald Ransom (New York: Grune and Strathon, 1976). pp. 23–38, esp. p. 26. Weakland also mentions the role of humor as a response exposing the incongruent nature of the double bind (p. 26), an observation that is not without relevance to Teresa's writing.

something the reverse of true humility. Can she really have thought herself a 'sea of evil,' a 'filthy scum,' 'the weakest and most wretched of all who have ever been born'? . . . We prefer to think that [these words] were penned in moments of depression or at seasons when her ardent love of God and her clear vision of His holiness made her write, passionately rather than reflectively, lines which she could never bring herself to erase.[15]

The opposite approach is to treat the self-depreciatory remarks as literary *topoi*. As Ernst Robert Curtius has shown, modesty formulas have a history as ancient as the Bible.[16] In classical rhetoric manuals the rationale for such expressions of "affected modesty" is the *captatio benevolentiae*, or the desire to dispose the reader favorably toward the writer. The modesty formulas could also be used to offset the presumption implied when the writer expressed the expertise that conferred on him the privilege to take up the pen. The following is a sampling of humility topics found in medieval and early Renaissance Spanish texts: the author is a sinner and inadequate to his literary task; it is only through divine intervention that he will be able to succeed; he writes under difficult conditions and therefore cannot produce a polished work; he writes only at the command of a superior or at the behest of friends; he bemoans his rustic speech; his work will doubtless require emendation by superior scholars.[17] Similar or identical ex-

[15] Peers, *Studies of the Spanish Mystics*, lst ed., 3 vols. (London: Sheldon, 1927), 1: 149–150.

[16] Curtius, *European Literature and the Latin Middle Ages*, trans. Willard R. Trask (1953; reprint ed., New York: Harper and Row, 1963), pp. 84–85.

[17] Margo De Ley, "The Prologue in Castilian Literature between 1200 and 1400" (Ph.D. diss., University of Illinois, 1976); Alberto Porqueras Mayo, *El prólogo en el Renacimiento español* (Madrid: Centro Superior de Investigaciones Científicas, 1965). Aurora Egido examines various topics in all of Teresa's prologues in the light of classical and Christian rhetorical traditions, concluding that many topics, though traditional, were personally motivated ("Los prólogos Teresianos y la 'Santa ignorancia,' " in *Con-*

pressions are found repeatedly in Teresa's *The Book of Her Life*. There are reiterated references to her bad memory, ignorance, stupidity, and foolishness; her physical weakness, wickedness, grave faults, and sins. She prays that God will give her the grace to write clearly and truthfully; she begs her reader to correct any errors and tear up anything that is foolish; she confesses that she is a silly little woman—a condition sufficient to "clip the wings" of any presumptuous aspirations: "Basta ser mujer para caérseme las alas, cuantimás mujer y ruin" (ch. 10, p. 45) 'Just being a woman is enough to have my wings fall off—how much more being both a woman and wretched as well' (K, 1: 77).

But even if we recognize a well-established rhetorical tradition for humility topics, we cannot assume that Teresa's topics have a traditional rhetorical function. Their frequency and distribution are something totally new. There are few humility topics in St. Augustine's *Confessions*. They are surprisingly rare in the devotional writers preferred by Teresa—Luis de Granada and Francisco de Osuna, for example. When topics do appear, they are found only in the prologue—that part of the text, which, after all, is devoted to the purpose of *captatio benevolentiae*. In contrast to the one or two humility topics found per prologue, Teresa's text offers two or three topics per page. In sum, we can only conclude that Teresa's position, as a woman and an ecstatic, was so precarious that she repeatedly needed to request the benevolent cooperation of her audience and at the same time "disavow her abilities and favors." *Captatio benevolentiae* was not a petrified tradition but a vital necessity. In this sense all of Teresa's works are *extended* prologues because, in her circumstances, the act of disavowing the privilege to write was of necessity conterminous with the act of claiming the privilege to write.[18]

---

greo internacional Teresiano 4–7 octubre, 1982, ed. Teófanes Egido Martínez et al. [Salamanca: Universidad de Salamanca, 1983], 2: 603.

[18] Teresa occasionally claimed the writer's privilege (the rhetorical *a causa*) in the headings to her chapters. It is notable that on at least one occasion her claim was scotched by her confessor. The last line of the

THE RHETORIC OF CONCESSION

The repeated humility topics do not begin to give us a complete picture of Teresa's rhetorical strategy. When we read Augustine's *Confessions*, we know what his sins were: theft, disobedience, and fornication. But although Teresa modeled the autobiographical parts of *The Book of Her Life* on the *Confessions*, she does not imitate Augustine's specificity about past sins. Teresa's confessions have a way of turning back upon themselves with so many qualifications, retractions, and hypothetical restatements that we sometimes lose track of the "core" confession. Some of her tactics could be described in classical rhetorical terms as variations on *concessio*. In traditional rhetorical manuals there are a number of devices that could be subsumed under the concept of concession: Quintilian's *praesumptio* or *prolepsis*, defined as anticipating "by confessing something we can afford to concede"; and Cicero's *praemunitio*, or defending "by anticipating objections to some point we propose to make later."[19] Although Teresa had never studied rhetoric, in an unsystematic fashion she may have absorbed from sermons or conversations with learned friends certain kinds of classical argumentative procedures. Whatever rhetorical lessons Teresa absorbed from a vigorous Renaissance oral culture, she assimilated them thoroughly. There is nothing programmatic about her persuasive strategy; with remarkable dexterity she engages in contradictory speech acts, pleading innocent and guilty at the same time. Conceding to the institutional authority of

---

heading for Chapter 18—"This should be read in a very subtle way and there are many noteworthy things"—was crossed out, probably by Báñez (K, 1: 293, n. 1). Adrienne Schizzano Mandel also argues that Teresa's self-derogation is part of a rhetorical strategy necessitated by her subordinate position as a female writer. See "El 'Yo' narrador en el *Libro de su vida* de Santa Teresa," in *La Chispa '85': Selected Proceedings*, ed. Gilbert Paolini (New Orleans: Tulane, 1985), pp. 231–242.

[19] See Lee A. Sonnino, *A Handbook to Sixteenth-Century Rhetoric* (New York: Barnes and Noble, 1968).

her confessors, she nevertheless carves out and defends inviolable areas of individual authority. She answers the paradoxical injunction to "prove her humility" with her own paradoxical rhetoric of concession.

Teresa's first confession is the story of her adolescent fall from virtue. Although she has inherited a natural inclination toward virtue from her parents, she has also been ambiguously blessed with natural attractiveness: "Comencé a entender las gracias de la naturaleza que el Señor me havía dado—que sigún decían eran muchas—, cuando por ellas le havía de dar gracias, de todas me comencé a ayudar para ofenderle, como ahora diré" (ch. 1, p. 18) 'When I began to know of the natural attractive qualities the Lord had bestowed on me (which others said were many), instead of thanking Him for them, I began to make use of them all to offend Him, as I shall now tell' (K, 1: 35).[20] She proceeds to explain how, as a sixteen-year-old motherless girl, she is obligated to entertain a flirtatious female relative and two male cousins. Somehow her honor is jeopardized because of these associations, and her father, Don Alonso de Cepeda, decides to send her away precipitously to an Augustinian convent that takes girls as boarders. The expulsion from home is surreptitious—the public explanation is: "porque haverse mi hermana casado, y quedar sola sin madre, no era bien" (ch. 2, p. 20) 'once my sister was married it seemed no longer good for me to stay at home without a mother' (K, 1: 37). The episode is ostensibly Teresa's female version of Augustine's confession of stealing the pears—an act that signals the adolescent's entry into the adult world of corruption. But let us see how this confessional act is embedded within other defensive acts:

> Y es ansí, que de tal manera me mudó esta conversación, que de natural y alma virtuoso, no me dejó casi ninguna, y

---

[20] Teresa indulges here in an untranslatable play on words: *gracias* meaning "graces" or "attractive qualities" as well as "thanks."

me parece me imprimía sus condiciones ella y otra que tenía la mesma manera de pasatiempos.

Por aquí entiendo el gran provecho que hace la buena compañía; y tengo por cierto que, si tratara en aquella edad con personas virtuosas, que estuviera entera en la virtud; porque si en esta edad tuviera quien me enseñara a temer a Dios, fuera tomando fuerzas el alma para no caer. Después, quitado este temor del todo, quedóme sólo el de la honra, que en todo lo que hacía me traía atormentada; con pensar que no se havía de saber, me atreavía [sic] a muchas cosas bien contra ella y contra Dios.

Al principio dañáronme las cosas dichas—a lo que me parece—, y no devía ser suya la culpa, sino mía; porque después mi malicia para el mal bastava, junto con tener criadas, que para todo mal hallava en ellas buen aparejo; que si alguna fuera en aconsejarme bien, por ventura me aprovechara; mas el interese les cegava, como a mí la afeción. Y pues nunca era inclinada a mucho mal—porque cosas deshonestas naturalmente las aborrecía—, sino a pasatiempos de buena conversación; mas puesta en la ocasión, estava en la mano el peligro, y ponía en él a mi padre y hermanos. De los cuales me libró Dios de manera que se parece bien procurava contra mi voluntad que del todo no me perdiese, aunque no pudo ser tan secreto que no huviese harta quiebra de mi honra y sospecha en mi padre. Porque no me parece havía tres meses que andava en estas vanidades, cuando me llevaron a un monesterio que havía en este lugar, adonde se criavan personas semejantes, aunque no tan ruines en costumbres como yo.   (ch. 2, pp. 19–20)

And indeed this conversation so changed me that hardly any virtue remained to my naturally virtuous soul. And I think she and another girl friend of the same type impressed their own traits upon me.

From such experiences I understand the great profit that comes from good companionship. And I am certain that if at that age I had gone around with virtuous persons, I would have remained whole in virtue. For should I have had when that age someone to teach me to fear God, my soul would have gained strength not to fall. Afterward, having lost this fear of God completely, I only had the fear of losing my reputation [honor], and such fear brought me torment in everything I did. With the thought that my deeds would not be known, I dared to do many things truly against my honor and against God.

These things did me harm, I think, at the beginning, and it wasn't her fault but mine. For afterward my malice was sufficient, together with having the maids around, for in them I found a helping hand for every kind of wrong. If there had been one of them to give me good counsel, I perhaps would have benefited by it; but self-interest blinded them as my vanity did me. I was never inclined to great evil—for I naturally abhorred indecent things—but to the pastime of pleasant conversation; yet, placed in the occasion, the danger was at hand, and my father's and brothers' reputation was in jeopardy as well. From all these occasions and dangers God delivered me in such a way that it seems clear He strove, against my will, to keep me from being completely lost, although this deliverance could not be achieved so secretly as to prevent me from suffering much loss of reputation and my father from being without suspicion. For it doesn't seem to me that three months during which I engaged in these vanities had gone by when my father brought me to a convent in that place where they educated persons like myself, although none with habits as [despicable] as mine.   (K, 1: 36–37)

In this passage confession alternates with self-exculpation. Teresa *confesses* to a change in character but attributes the responsibility for her moral transformation to the pernicious influence of the frivolous girlfriend. The theme of "the necessity of good companions for children" might count as a parenthetical piece of advice, but it also carries an implicit criticism of her own father, who feared offending a relative and refused to put an end to the girlfriend's visits. Although Teresa now returns to the confessional mode (saying she had lost her fear of God), its force is somewhat mitigated by her acknowledgment that she still was concerned for her honor—that sense of propriety in regard to a social and sexual reputation. She comes closest to an admission of sin when she confesses that she did many things thinking that no one would find out about them, but these "many things" are still unspecified.

Reverting to the theme of "bad company" in the third paragraph, Teresa retracts the blame previously placed on the female relative, confessing self-sufficiency for her sins. But the confession is immediately qualified by "together with having the maids round." The defense of "pernicious influence" has *not* been abandoned but rather the blame has been shifted from the girlfriend to the servants. Teresa now proposes a hypothesis that again redounds negatively upon Don Alonso: if bad company had led her into sin, good advice would have kept her from sinning. She confesses that the situation was ripe with danger for her family's honor. One of Teresa's most recent biographers has assumed that this is a confession of loss of virginity.[21] But Teresa states quite specifically that God Himself prevented the actual occurrence of sin. Although her subsequent expulsion from her father's home is related as a *punishment* for her "vanities," the final self-inculpating *ruin* ("despicable") is resoundingly insubstantial.

What Teresa's "despicable habits" amount to is having been placed, against her will, in a situation in which sexual misconduct or the *appearance* of misconduct could have taken place. The only misconduct she is at all specific about is having resisted temptation for the wrong reason: she was concerned for her honor.[22] At issue, then, is a "so-

[21] Victoria Lincoln, *Teresa: A Woman. A Biography of Teresa de Avila*, ed. Elias Rivers and Antonio de Nicolás (Albany: State University of New York Press, 1984).

[22] This passage also reflects Teresa's awareness of the controversy surrounding contrition versus attrition that was a major topic at the Council of Trent. The theologians at Trent attempted to salvage the doctrine of imperfect confession, or attrition, which the Protestants had impugned

cial" sin— the loss of the appearance of virtue—that is resisted largely because of "social" motives. This, accompanied by a generic confession of despicability, takes the place of a confession of a specified sin. Teresa thus salvages her innocence with a rhetorical *concessio*, while she complies with the command to "confess all."

ALTERNATIVE NARRATIVES

But Teresa is not simply pleading guilty to lesser charges in this chapter: a covert message of protest directed against her father is concealed in the inexplicable contradictions surrounding the narrative. Teresa had endangered her father's honor; he therefore sent her away to a convent school. Nonetheless, she insists: "Era tan demasiado el amor que mí padre me tenía y la mucha disimulación mía, que no havía creer tanto mal de mí, y ansí no quedó en desgracia conmigo" (ch. 2, p. 20) 'So excessive was the love my father bore me and so great my dissimulation that he was unable to believe there was much wrong with me, and so he was not angered with me' (K, 1: 37).[23] Later still she asserts that the questionable relationship was really nothing more than a broken engagement.[24] Has she not been punished both for being the exclusive

---

as hypocrisy. Attrition was conceived as motivated by fear of punishment rather than love of God but was nevertheless held to be an effect of grace and sufficient for justification. Teresa "confesses" to attrition here and at the end of Chapter 5.

[23] In an illuminating article Gari Laguardia analyses the significance of Teresa's ambivalent love for her father and the reproaches against him implied in her confession ("Santa Teresa and the Problem of Desire," *Hispania* 63 [1980]: 523–530).

[24] "Una cosa tenía que parece me podía ser alguna disculpa—si no tuviera tantas culpas—, y es que era el trato con quien por vía de casamiento me parecía podía acabar en bien" (ch. 2, p. 20) 'One thing, it seems, that could have amounted to some excuse for me, should I not have had so many faults, was that the friendship with one of my cousins was in view of a possible marriage' (K, 1: 38).

woman in her father's life (the public reason for her expulsion) and for wishing to break away through marriage? Don Alonso, in fact, never intended for Teresa to become a nun, and when in 1533 she declared her religious vocation, he refused to grant her his permission to take the veil: "Era tanto lo que me quería, que en ninguna manera lo pude acabar con él, ni bastaron ruegos de personas que procuré le hablasen; lo que más se pudo acabar con él, fue que después de sus días haría lo que quisiese" (ch. 3, p. 22) 'So great was his love for me that in no way was I able to obtain his permission or achieve anything through persons I asked to intercede for me. The most we could get from him was that after his death I could do whatever I wanted' (K 1: 40). In 1535 Teresa once again left home, secretly escaping at night to the Carmelite Convent of the Incarnation in Avila. The internal struggle between love of God and love of father is intense: "[C]uando salí de casa de mi padre, no creo será más el sentimiento cuando me muera; porque me parece cada hueso se me apartava por sí" (ch. 4, p. 22) '[W]hen I left my father's house I felt the separation so keenly that the feeling will not be greater, I think, when I die. For it seemed that every bone in my body was being sundered' (K, 1: 41). Only God's help, giving her "courage against herself," allowed her to achieve the necessary "detachment for God alone" (K, 1: 41). The terror (*espanto*) of disobedience, Teresa explains, was actually a trial sent from God so that her soul might gain "more merit." Thus, by presenting the second separation between father and daughter as a reluctant act of obedience to a higher authority, Teresa writes an alternative history that redresses the injustice of her earlier expulsion.

Teresa returns to a narrative of painful detachment in Chapter 4. Once again the story entails both confession and protest. In 1537, after two years in the Convent of the Incarnation, Teresa's health had been ruined. That winter her father removed her from the convent and brought her to the town of Becedas where she would be treated for her illness. During this period she began to confess with a priest who became inordinately fond of her: "No fue la afeción de éste mala, mas de demasiada afeción venía a no ser buena" (ch. 5, p. 26) 'His affection for me was not bad; but since it was too great, it came to no good' (K, 1: 47). In fact, the priest was so moved by Teresa's youth and virtue that, inverting their hierarchical position, he began to confess to his confessional daughter.[25] Teresa thus discovered that the priest was in thrall to his mistress, whose copper amulet he wore around his neck: "Pues, como supe esto, comencé a mostrarle más amor. Mi intención buena era, la obra mala; pues por hacer bien, por grande que sea, no havía de hacer un pequeño mal. Tratávale muy ordinario de Dios; esto devía aprovecharle, aunque más creo le hizo al caso el quererme mucho; porque por hacerme placer me vino a dar el idolillo, el cual hice echar luego en un río" (ch. 5, p. 27) 'Once I knew about these charms, I began to show him more love. My intention was good; the deed was bad. For in order to do good, no matter how great, one should not commit the slightest wrong. I used to speak with him very often about God. This must have profited him, although I rather believe that it prompted him to love me greatly. For in order to please me, he finally gave me the little idol, which I then threw in a river' (K, 1: 48). The priest thereupon experienced a spiritual awakening that allowed him to break with his mistress. Exactly one year from the day he met Teresa he died an exemplary Christian death.

Once again a narrative is manipulated by Teresa to count as a confession of a situation in which sin could have occurred but didn't: "[A]quella afición grande que me tenía, nunca entendí ser mala, aunque pudiera ser con más puridad; mas también huvo ocasiones para que, si no se tuviera muy delante a Dios, huviera ofensas suyas más graves" (ch. 5, p. 27) 'I never thought that the great affection he bore me was wrong, although it could have been

---

[25] Laguardia writes, "Teresa assumes the role of confessor, as well as of 'lover' " ("Santa Teresa and the Problem of Desire," p. 525).

more pure. But there were also occasions on which, if we had not remained very much in God's presence, there would have been more serious offenses' (K, 1: 48). But the narrative's subtext defends Teresa's actions as a good deed, though imperfectly executed. In essence, Teresa uses her beneficent charm ("por hacerme placer" 'to please me') to combat the malevolent charm (idolillo 'the little idol') of the priest's mistress. Thus, with her imagined role as benevolent seductress who wins back a soul for God she rewrites her actual history as coquette.

In spite of the happy ending to this episode Teresa discovered that once she returned to the Incarnation the conflict between human friendships and friendship with God—as she defined mental prayer—became intensified. Following the custom at the Incarnation, Teresa frequently received outside visitors. Eventually a particular friendship began to trouble her greatly. Once while engaged in conversation with this unnamed person she reports that she saw a large toad moving quickly toward them—an event that she took as a sign of God's displeasure over her secular friendships. The affection she inspired in other nuns only increased her sense of unworthiness for God's affection. As a result, she decided to give up mental prayer. The following passage, though long, is particularly revealing if we are willing to follow the interwoven strands of confession and protest.

Pues ansí comencé de pasatiempo en pasatiempo, de vanidad en vanidad, de ocasión en ocasión, a meterme tanto en muy grandes ocasiones y andar tan estragada mi alma en muchas vanidades, que ya yo tenía vergüenza de en tan particular amistad como es tratar de oración, tornarme a llegar a Dios. . . . Este fue el más terrible engaño que el demonio me podía hacer debajo de parecer humildad: que comencé a temer de tener oración, de verme tan perdida; y parecíame era mijor andar como los muchos—pues en ser ruin era de los peores—y rezar lo que estava obligada, y vocalmente, que no tener oración mental y tanto trato con Dios la que merecía estar con los demonios, y que engañava a la gente, porque en lo esterior tenía buenas apariencias. Y ansí no es de culpar a la casa donde estava, porque con mi maña procurava me tuviesen en buena opinión—aunque no de advertencia—fingiendo cristiandad; porque en esto de hiproquesía [sic] y vanagloria, gloria a Dios, jamás me acuerdo haverle ofendido—que yo entienda; . . . Por ventura si Dios primitiera me tentara en esto tan recio como en otras cosas, también cayera; . . . antes me pesava mucho de que me tuviesen en buena opinión, como yo sabía lo secreto de mí.

Este no me tener por tan ruin venía que, como me vían tan moza y en tantas ocasiones, y apartarme muchas veces a soledad a rezar y leer mucho, hablar de Dios, amiga de hacer pintar su imagen en muchas partes, y de tener oratorio y procurar en él cosas que hiciesen devoción, no decir mal, otras cosas de esta suerte que tenían apariencia de virtud— y yo que de vana me sabía estimar en las cosas que el mundo se suelen tener por estima.   (ch. 7, pp. 31–32)

Since I thus began to go from pastime to pastime, from vanity to vanity, from one occasion to another, to place myself so often in very serious occasions, and to allow my soul to become so spoiled by many vanities, I was then ashamed to return to the search for God by means of a friendship as special as is that found in the intimate exchange of prayer. . . . This was the most terrible trick the devil could play on me, under the guise of humility: that seeing myself so corrupted I began to fear the practice of prayer. It seemed to me that, since in being wicked I was among the worst, it was better to go the way of the many, to recite what I was obliged to vocally and not to practice mental prayer and so much intimacy with God, for I merited to be with the devils. And it seemed to me that I was deceiving people since exteriorly I kept up such good appearances. Thus the convent where I resided was not at fault. For in my craftiness I strove to be held in esteem, although I did not advertently feign Christianity. In this matter of hypocrisy and vainglory, praise God, I don't recall ever having offended Him knowingly. . . . Perhaps if God had permitted me to be tempted in this regard as severely as in other things, I would also have fallen. . . . Rather, I grieved very much over being held in esteem since I knew what was down deep in my heart.

The fact that they did not consider me so bad was due to their seeing me so young and in the midst of so many occasions, often withdrawing into solitude to pray and read, speaking much about God, fond of having His image painted and put up in many places and of having an oratory and seeking in it the things that promote devotion, not engaging in fault-finding or other things of this sort that have the appearance of virtue.   (K, 1: 55–56)

As in the previous passage the total contextual effect is more than the sum of its parts. Teresa's problem is to explain that her abandonment of suspect mental prayer for Counter-Reformation oral prayer constituted, in fact, a second fall. Furthermore, this lapse was caused, at least in part, by the distractions of the uncloistered life at the Convent of the Incarnation. She must do this without appearing ungrateful, arrogant, or critical of the nuns who were her superiors. She begins, therefore, by explicitly taking the blame for the distracting liberties that were granted to her, but by doing so she opens herself to the charge of hypocrisy. This anticipated charge is explicitly denied and replaced with a *hypothetical* confession ("perhaps I would also have fallen"). The catalogue of actions that follows (praying, reading, devotion to images of Christ) counts as a confession, since these activities obscured Teresa's "wickedness" from her superiors. But they are nevertheless done without hypocrisy and vainglory: they are the visible acts of Counter-Reformation piety that were defended and promoted at the Council of Trent. On the contextual level the statement must stand as a defense, while the blame for granting Teresa excessive liberty is projected onto the nuns in authority, who had *misread* Teresa's behavior as proof that she was exempt from temptation and whose excessive fondness for her was a hindrance to her spiritual progress.

The question of temptation raises another paradox, for Teresa did in fact confirm the nuns' good opinion of her. In spite of the liberty granted to her, as she goes on to explain, she never engaged in such illicit behavior as "giving messages through holes in the walls, or at night" (K, 1: 56). Although she is careful to deny that sisters in her particular convent were guilty of similar actions, the idea nevertheless stands as an implicit comparison. The segment as a whole establishes a comparison between Teresa, who committed unspecified sins unintentionally, and other unspecified nuns who commit specific sins intentionally. Her superiors' good opinion of her, like Osuna's "attention which offends Humility," must be disavowed, but it is nonetheless legitimate: Teresa is innocent of any sin her superiors would have been concerned with but guilty of abandoning mental prayer. Her "wickedness" is of an order that falls outside of the jurisdiction and comprehension of her earthly judges; it is a question of her intimate relationship with God.

In her attempt to explain the conflict between human relationships and mental prayer as an exclusive friendship with God, Teresa inevitably returns to the theme of her relationship with her father. Don Alonso was the one to oversee her treatment at Becedas—a devastating regime of daily purges that further destroyed her precarious health. When Don Alonso refused to allow Teresa to confess, believing that she was unnecessarily alarmed about her health, Teresa fell into a coma that lasted four days and brought her to the brink of death. At this point her indictment of her father is unveiled: "¡Oh amor de carne demasiado, que aunque sea de tan católico padre y tan avisado—que lo era harto, que no fue ignorancia—me pudiera hacer gran daño!" (ch. 5, pp. 27–28) '[Oh, too fleshly love], even though from so Catholic and prudent a father (for he was every bit of this, and his action did not arise from ignorance), it could have done me great harm!'

(K, 1: 49). Once again her father's possessive love has been an obstacle to Teresa's well-being—this time it has nearly resulted in her spiritual and physical death.

Nonetheless, after Teresa recovered from the paralysis brought on by the Becedas cure, she began to instruct Don Alonso in mental prayer, and he soon became an advanced practitioner. But when Teresa gave up contemplation, he withdrew from her in disappointment: "[Mi padre] me huvo lástima. Mas como él estava ya en tan subido estado, no estava después tanto conmigo, sino, como me havía visto, ívase, que decía era tiempo perdido; como yo le gastava en otras vanidades, dávaseme poco" (ch. 7, p. 34) '[My father] pitied me. But since he had already reached so sublime a state, he did not afterward spend as much time with me but would leave after a brief visit; for he said it was time lost. Since I wasted time on other vanities, I cared little about losing time' (K, 1: 61). Again the confession conceals a protest. After describing at length the external pressures, illness, and unwarranted scruples that undermined her dedication to the contemplative life, she reveals that her father—her disciple in prayer—withdrew the affection she needed to sustain her during a period of spiritual aridity.

Even within the walls of the Incarnation Teresa had found herself trapped between unviable alternatives. Her attempts to forge nonpaternal emotional attachments had only redounded in more sexual guilt. Yet a spiritual relationship with her father, based on the mutual practice of mental prayer and the reconciliation it brought, was still troubling. Teresa consequently chose to abandon mental prayer—and her father. Ironically, the second fall (like the second "expulsion" from home) was a *fortunate* fall, which allowed her finally to loosen the ties of her father's "too fleshly" love. Only after Don Alonso's death, as we shall see, would Teresa obtain the "freedom" to enjoy reciprocal human affection.

The pattern that emerges—the story that must be told and retold—is one of attraction and detachment. Human love is a double bind, for feminine virtue is attractive, and the line between attraction and seduction lies in the eyes of the beholder. Teresa confesses to her attractiveness—her unwitting power to inspire love and confidence in others—but insists on the inadequacy of their love, their idealizing demands on her, and her painful efforts to free herself from those affective ties.

In *The Book of Her Life* Teresa executes speech acts whose *force* is confessional: she repeatedly asserts that she performed certain actions and expresses sorrow for them, and does so within an institutional hierarchy that gives ritual significance to the conjunction of such verbal acts. But the rhetorical *effect* is defensive. Her strategy of conceding to lesser sins allows her, on the theological level, to defend her right to practice mental prayer and, on a personal level, to protest that others have loved her, not wisely, but too well.

CAPTATIO BENEVOLENTIAE

We have seen how Teresa responds to different strands of her paradoxical injunction at different levels of the speech act. Another aspect of her creative disentanglement involves her ability to gain a measure of control over the speech situation. The fact that she writes out of obedience would seem to indicate that she, like the prototypic subject of a double bind, is in a controlled communicative situation from which there is "no exit"—no possibility of clarification or redress. But in spite of the dependence and intensity of the penitent/confessor relationship Teresa does not accept the writer/reader relationship as static. Rather, she continually reshapes it in ways that subvert hierarchy and allow her greater flexibility of expression.

We would expect that Teresa's discourse should be strongly marked by the verbal strategies subordinates use when addressing their superiors. And indeed many aspects of the text's *captatio benevolentiae* could be considered as manifestations of conventional deference. But Teresa also employs speech acts that are much more characteristic of discourse between persons with close ties and similar rank. The behavioral theory developed by sociolinguists Penelope Brown and Stephen Levinson is particularly useful for examining Teresa's "mixed" linguistic strategy. "Politeness," according to this model, is a "rational, strategic . . . behavior, . . . predicting the kinds of linguistic strategies which will be employed in particular circumstances."[26] "Negative politeness" is motivated by the speaker's desire not to interfere with the addressee's freedom of action and is characterized by self-effacement, formality, restraint, self-disparagement, and acknowledgment of the addressee's rank and authority. For example, specific features such as performance hedges ("Perhaps," "I think"), depersonalizing mechanisms ("Someone might think"), and indirect speech acts ("It's cold in here?" for "Close the window!") might contribute to the aim of distancing and nonimposing, which defines negative politeness.[27] "Positive politeness," on the other hand, is motivated by the speaker's willingness to comply with the addressee's desires "to be liked, admired, and ratified"[28] and emphasizes shared values and attitudes, stressing the speaker's understanding and appreciation of the addressee. Brown and Levinson observed in a number of social groups that emphatic particles together with irony, joking, fictive kin terms, and inclusive "we" pronouns contributed to the aim of a positively polite conversational style.[29]

[26] Penelope Brown, "How and Why Are Women More Polite: Some Evidence from a Mayan Community," in *Women and Language in Literature and Society*, ed. Sally McConnell-Ginet, Ruth Borker, and Nelly Furman (New York: Praeger, 1980), pp. 111–136, quotation p. 114. A more extensive presentation of the model is found in Brown and Levinson, "Universals in Language Usage: Politeness Phenomena," in *Questions and Politeness: Strategies in Social Interaction*, ed. Esther Goody (Cambridge: At the University Press, 1978), pp. 56–289.

[27] Brown, "How and Why," pp. 128–129.

[28] Ibid., p. 115.

[29] Ibid., pp. 128–129; Brown and Levinson, "Universals," pp. 113, 129.

Coming as she did from a society with a sharp dichotomy between male and female power, Teresa's ability to mix a strategy of formality and subordination with one of intimacy and solidarity is especially remarkable. This strategic maneuverability is particularly apparent when Teresa singles out Father García de Toledo as her principal addressee. García's role as interlocutor in *The Book of Her Life* requires some explanation of its rather complicated textual history. Before Teresa actually began to write the history of her life, she had already written various fragmentary accounts of her past, the supernatural phenomena experienced, and her method of prayer for confessors, advisors, and theologians whose support she solicited. The content of these accounts was eventually incorporated into one text prepared for her current confessor, García de Toledo, in 1562. This text was in turn expanded and revised between 1564 and 1565, to include an account of the founding of the first reformed Carmelite convent. Although García de Toledo became her primary addressee—she refers to him as "vuestra merced" (your grace)—she occasionally reverts to the plural "vuestras mercedes" as a gesture of recognition, perhaps, to those reading over García de Toledo's shoulder.[30] The existence of multiple addressees and the variety of Teresa's rhetorical strategies in adjusting to them has as its consequence a particularly polymorphous autobiographical "I" and an equally elusive writer/reader relationship. The phantoms of earlier addressees undoubtedly persist in the "definitive" version of her text; the degree of authority and her feelings of intimacy vary with her addressees; the possibility of yet unknown readers, especially Inquisitorial examiners, surely exists in the

---

[30] For a detailed description of the textual history of *Libro de la vida* see Enrique Llamas-Martínez, "El libro de la vida," in *Introducción a la lectura de Santa Teresa*, ed. Alberto Barrientos et al. (Madrid: Editorial de espiritualidad, 1978), pp. 210–219. Víctor García de la Concha explores in depth Teresa's adaptation to an ever-widening circle of addressees (*El arte literario de Santa Teresa* [Barcelona: Ariel, 1978], pp. 190–227).

background of the intimate "you and I" reader pact.[31] Nevertheless, it is possible to make some assumptions about her use of García de Toledo as a primary reader/confessor and about her attempts to reduce the hierarchical distance between them.

Teresa had encountered García de Toledo while she was staying with the widow Doña Luisa de la Cerda in Toledo in 1562. She writes that she had seen him attending mass at St. Peter the Martyr and felt impelled to "know the state of his soul." Three times she began but hesitated before she approached him and interrupted his prayer. In the months that followed Teresa prayed fervently that her new confidant might be converted to the practice of mental prayer. She thus won a "friend" for God and was in fact astonished at García's rapid progress (ch. 34). García de Toledo's friendship came at a crucial time. Her confessor, Alvarez, had strenuously opposed her efforts to found the new convent in Avila, while her ally, Father Ibáñez, had withdrawn to a solitary monastery. For a period Te-

---

[31] Much more could be said about Teresa's manipulation of her readers. Sol Villacèque explains how Teresa opens up a closed communcative situation in the Prologue ("Rhetorique et Pragmatique," pp. 7–27). Frances Matos Schultz has written persuasively of Teresa's achievement in dismantling a monolithic ideological Authority into lesser grades of true and false authorities ("Autoridad e ideología en el *Libro de la Vida* de Santa Teresa de Jesús," *Atenea* 2 [1982]: 41–48). She also emphasizes the significance of García de Toledo as a principal addressee, especially after Chapter 10. Mary C. Sullivan argues that Teresa was increasingly concerned with directing her discourse toward a "creative self-projection of readers" in "From Narrative to Proclamation: A Rhetorical Analysis of the Autobiography of Teresa of Avila," *Thought* 58 (1983): 453–471; quotation p. 459. Aurora Egido argues that Teresa's voluntary multiplication of interlocutors—including misreaders like the *letrados*—enriches her work ("Santa Teresa contra los letrados: Los interlocutores en su obra," *Criticón* 20 [1982]: 85–121). Taking the opposite point of view, Antonio Carreño has written that Teresa was so overwhelmed by trying to satisfy the conflicting demands of multiple readers that her narrative voice, her "Yo," became entirely fictive ("Las paradojas del 'Yo' autobiográfico," *Santa Teresa y la literature mística hispánica*, ed. Manuel Criado de Val, [Madrid: EDI–6, 1984], pp. 255–264).

resa could not find anyone who dared to hear her confession. But in García she found not only her confessional father but a spiritual son. When García ordered her to give a complete account of her spiritual life, as penitent her obligation was to remember and confess all her transgressions; but as *his* spiritual teacher she felt she had the right to demand his devotion and *his* humility in accepting her spiritual guidance. Hierarchy is confused and diminished by the oxymoronic role he is given in the text; he is made to share the injunction to prove his humility:

> ¡Oh hijo mío! (que es tan humilde, que ansí se quiere nombrar a quien va esto dirigido y me lo mandó escrivir). . . . Suplico a vuestra merced seamos todos locos por amor de quien por nosotros se lo llamaron. Pues dice vuesa merced que me quiere, en disponerse para que Dios le haga esta merced quiero que me lo muestre; porque veo muy pocos que no los vea con seso demasiado para lo que les cumple. Ya puede ser que tenga yo más que todos; no me lo consienta vuestra merced, padre mío, pues también lo es como hijo, pues es mi confesor y a quien he fiado mi alma.
>
> (ch. 16, p. 66)

> Oh my son! (The one to whom this is addressed and who ordered me to write this is so humble that he wants to be so called.) . . . I beg of your Reverence that we may all be mad for love of Him who for love of us was called mad. Since your Reverence says that you love me, prove it to me by preparing yourself so that God may grant you this favor; I see very few who do not have much more discretion than is necessary for their spiritual progress. It could well be that I am the one who abounds in this more than all others. Don't allow this to happen to me, my father (since you are also like a son), for you are my confessor and the one to whom I have entrusted my soul.
>
> (K, 1: 111)[32]

---

[32] Dámaso Chicharro observes in his edition to *Libro de la vida* (Madrid: Cátedra, 1979) that the phrase "hijo mío" has been scored in the manuscript and concludes that Teresa herself modified the phrase in revision, perhaps because it seemed too emotional (p. 237, n. 23).

García de Toledo also becomes an intermediary between the writer and other potentially hostile readers. He is a premodern editor, entrusted with all the prerogatives of emendation or deletion. Nowhere is the intimacy of this relationship more obvious than at the end of Chapter 7:

No sé si digo desatinos; si lo son, vuestra merced los rompa; y si no lo son, le suplico ayude a mi simpleza con añidir aquí mucho; porque andan ya las cosas del servicio de Dios tan flacas que es menester hacerse espaldas unos a otros los que le sirven, para ir adelante . . . y si uno comienza a darse a Dios, hay tantos que mormuren, que es menester buscar compañía para defenderse, hasta que ya estén fuertes en no les pesar de padecer, y si no, veránse en mucho aprieto; . . . Y *es un género de humildad no fiar de sí, sino creer que para aquellos con quien conversa le ayudará Dios;* y crece la caridad con ser comunicada, y hay mil bienes que no los osaría decir, si no tuviese gran espiriencia de lo mucho que va en esto.

Verdad es que yo soy más flaca y ruin que todos los nacidos; mas creo no perderá quien *humillándose—aunque sea fuerte—*no lo crea de sí y creyere en esto a quien tiene espiriencia. (ch. 7, p. 37, my emphasis)

I don't know if I am speaking foolish words. If I am, may your Reverence tear them up; and if they are not, help my stupidity by adding here a great deal. There is so much sluggishness in matters having to do with the service of God that it is necessary for those who serve Him to become shields for one another that they might advance. . . . If someone begins to give himself to God, there are so many to criticize him that he needs to seek companionship to defend himself until he is so strong that it is no longer a burden for him to suffer this criticism. . . .

And it is a kind of humility not to trust in oneself but to believe that through those with whom one converses God will help and increase charity while it is being shared. And there are a thousand graces I would not dare speak of if I did not have powerful experience of the benefit that comes from this sharing.

It is true that I am the weakest and most wicked of all human beings. But I believe he will not be lost who, *humbling himself, even though he be strong*, does not believe by himself but believes this one who has experience.

(K, 1: 64–65, my emphasis)

In this passage Teresa shifts back and forth between negative and positive politeness strategies with bewildering dexterity. Although she begins with the self-disparagement characteristic of negative politeness, she switches to the strategy of positive politeness when she alludes to the common danger facing practitioners of mental prayer. The derogatory remarks about nonpractitioners of prayer (their spiritual "sluggishness") also serves to reinforce ingroup cohesiveness—another characteristic of positive politeness. But when Teresa dares to give advice to her superior, she reverts to the negative politeness strategy of impersonalization ("It is a kind of humility not to trust in *oneself*"). Teresa's egalitarian acts of advising and flattering in the last paragraph are again bracketed by the negative politeness strategies of self-depreciation and impersonalization.

Although Teresa knew that inevitably there would be other readers of her text in addition to García, she frequently devised ways to subvert the public nature of her discourse. In Chapter 34 she describes the spiritual progress of "a certain Dominican father" (García himself) who, in a very short time, began to receive favors from mental prayer. A hypothetical *letrado* (someone, we can infer, very much like her troublesome confessor Alvarez) might be skeptical of this rapid progress. But, she argues, favors do not derive from absolute perfection or years spent in prayer. She slyly suggests that such an inexperienced *letrado* could learn a lesson in humility from a *viejecita* or "little old woman."

Teresa goes on to relate a "powerful rapture" that occurred during a conversation with "the Dominican father": "Vi a Cristo con grandísima majestad y gloria mostrando gran contento de lo que allí pasava, y ansí me lo dijo y quiso viese claro que a semejantes pláticas siempre se hallava presente y lo mucho que se sirve en que ansí se deleiten en hablar en El" (ch. 34, p. 144) 'I saw Christ with awesome majesty and glory showing great happiness over what was taking place. Thus He told me and wanted me to see clearly that He was always present in conversations like these and how much He is pleased when persons so delight in speaking of Him' (K, 1: 234). Through this vision, in stark contrast to the vision of the enormous toad, we see that Christ is not so much the addressee as the witness who authorizes the intimacy of the discourse. With García de Toledo Teresa could claim the freedom to accept a reciprocal emotional bond, ensconced within a divine triangle.[33] Teresa's "coded" flattery of García, the private references to their shared experiences and common opponent, all serve to re-create an exclusive conversation with an intimate other—an intimacy that is reassuringly presided over and sanctioned by Christ.

A reiterated complaint of Teresa's is that she has been *misread*—by her father, the nuns at the Incarnation, the priest of Becedas, by her earlier skeptical confessors and unnamed *letrados*. All of these "readers" have placed her in a double bind by requiring her to defend their exalted expectations of her virtue. By claiming García de Toledo as her ally, by making him share her perspective as a potential victim of persecution, by defining humility not as a demand imposed from above but a shared value, she undermines his status as adversary and critic. He is transformed from the addressee who sets the terms for the binding discourse into an ideal reader, the *chosen* reader, receptive to Teresa's self-evaluation and self-justification.

[33] Teresa refers explicitly to this freedom in a revealing passage in Chapter 37. She confesses a "serious fault"—a tendency toward strong attachments. But after a vision of Christ she was free of fear that such affection might be excessive.

FALSE HUMILITY

We have seen that through a rhetoric of concession and appeal to a benevolent reader Teresa has attempted to respond to the contradictory strands of a paradoxical injunction. In the course of her confessional autobiography she also approaches the double bind more directly, when she attempts to *define* the paradoxical demands placed on her. The focus of this metacommunicative task is, once more, the concept of humility. As Teresa struggled to express her second "fall," as we have seen, the queen of Christian virtues began to acquire negative markers: "seeming" humility was responsible for her abandonment of mental prayer, and the fear of vainglory was in fact a stratagem (*ardid*) of the devil. Teresa goes on to argue that abandoning mental prayer or friendships with other practitioners of prayer because of this scruple would be as absurd as avoiding mass: "El que de hablar en esto tuviere vanagloria, también la terná en oír misa con devoción, si le ven, y en hacer otras cosas que, so pena de no ser cristiano, las ha de hacer, y no se han de dejar por miedo de vanagloria" (ch. 7, p. 36) 'Anyone who is afraid of falling into vainglory by speaking of these things should also fear being seen attending mass with devotion and doing other things he must do if he wants to be Christian and must not be abandoned for fear of vainglory' (my translation).

Repeatedly she advises the practitioners of prayer to beware of this "temptation" of humility which arises when one tries too hard to please earthly authorities:

No cure de unas humildades que hay . . . que les parece humildad no entender que el Señor les va dando dones. Entendamos bien, bien, como ello es, que nos los da Dios sin ningún merecimiento nuestro, y agradezcámoslo a Su Majestad; porque si no conocemos que recibimos, no nos despertamos a amar.

Y es cosa muy cierta, que mientras más vemos estamos ricos, sobre conocer somos pobres, más aprovechamiento nos viene y aún más *verdadera humildad*. Lo demás es acovardar el ánimo a parecer que no es capaz de grandes bienes si en comenzando el Señor a dárselos comienza él a atemorizarse con miedo de vanagloria. Creamos que quien nos da los bienes, nos dará gracia para que, en comenzando el demonio a tentarle en este caso, lo entienda, y fortaleza para resistir; digo, si andamos con llaneza delante de Dios, pretendiendo contentar sólo a El, *y no a los hombres*.

(ch. 10, p. 44, my emphasis)

Let him pay no attention to the kind of humility . . . in which it seems to some that it is humility not to acknowledge that God is giving them gifts. Let us understand most clearly the real fact: God gives them to us without any merit on our part. And let us thank His Majesty for them, because, if we do not acknowledge we are receiving them, we will not awaken ourselves to love. And it is very certain that while we see more clearly that we are rich, over and above knowing that we are poor, more benefit comes to us, and even more *authentic humility*. Anything else would amount to intimidating the spirit, making it believe that it isn't capable of great blessings, so that when the Lord begins to give them to it, it starts to get frightened about vainglory. Let us believe that He who gives us the blessings will give us the grace so that when the devil begins to tempt us in this way we shall understand and have the fortitude to resist—I mean, if we walk with sincerity before God, aiming at pleasing Him alone *and not men*.   (K, 1: 75, my emphasis)

In contradistinction to these seeming "humilities" (*unas humildades*) that are in fact a form of cowardice an oxymoronic "bold" humility emerges: "Quiere su Majestad, y es amigo de ánimas animosas, como vayan con humildad y nunca confianza de sí" (ch. 13, p. 53) 'His Majesty wants this determination, and He is a friend of courageous souls if they walk in humility and without trusting in self' (K, 1: 89); "Y ansí ruego yo, por amor del Señor, a las almas a quien Su Majestad ha hecho tan gran merced de que lleguen a este estado, que se conozcan y tengan en mucho, *con una humilde y santa presunción* para no tornar a las ollas de Egito" (ch. 15, p. 61) 'Thus, for the love of the Lord, I beg those whom His Majesty has so highly favored in the attainment of this state that they understand it and esteem it *with a humble and holy [presumptuousness]* so as not to return to the fleshpots of Egypt' (K, 1: 103, my emphasis).

By splitting humility into a true and a counterfeit virtue Teresa has effectively answered her opponents' accusation of vainglory. Her narrative also makes clear that she needed to defend herself not only from external accusation but internalized doubts as well, for humility is a particularly subtle and devastating temptation.

The lines of inner conflict are most forcefully described in chapters 30 to 35. These describe the period of extreme spiritual distress and controversy surrounding her efforts to found the Convent of St. Joseph's, exacerbated by the opposition of the Carmelite provincial as well as the open hostility of the city and many of the nuns of her own community at the Incarnation. Overcome with depression she was inclined to believe the charges against her: "Parecíame yo tan mala que cuantos males y herejías les habían levantado me parecía eran por mis pecados" (ch. 30, p. 121) 'It seemed to me I was so evil that all the wickedness and heresies that had arisen were due to my sins' (K, 1: 197). But with hindsight she is able to articulate the paradoxical demands of the double bind in terms of true versus false humility:

> Esta es una humilad falsa que el demonio inventava para desasosegarme y provar si puede traer el alma a desesperación. Tengo ya tanta espiriencia que es cosa del demonio, que, como ya ve que le entiendo, no me atormenta en esto tantas veces como solía. Vese claro en la inquietud y desasosiego con que comienza y el alboroto que da el alma todo lo que dura, y la escuridad y aflición que en ella pone, la sequedad y mala dispusición para oración ni para ningún bien. Parece que ahoga el alma y ata el cuerpo para que de nada aproveche.   (ch. 30, p. 121)

This was a false humility the devil invented in order to disquiet me and try, if he could, to bring my soul to despair. I have so much experience now of when something is from the devil that since he at present sees that I understand him, he doesn't torment me in this way as often as he used to. He is recognized clearly by the disturbance and disquiet with which he begins, by the agitation the soul feels as long as his works last, by the darkness and affliction he places in the soul, and by dryness and the disinclination toward prayer or toward any good work. (K, 1: 197)

In contrast, she defines true humility as follows:

[P]orque la humildad verdadera (aunque se conoce el alma por ruin y da pena ver lo que somos . . .) no viene con alboroto, ni desasosiega el alma ni la escurece, ni da sequedad, antes la regala, y es todo a el revés: con quietud, con suavidad, con luz . . . duélele lo que ofendió a Dios, por otra parte la ensancha su misericordia. (ch. 30, p. 121)

Even though the soul knows its own wretchedness and grieves to see what we are, . . . true humility doesn't come to the soul with agitation or disturbance, nor does it darken it or bring it dryness. Rather, true humility consoles and acts in a completely opposite way: quietly, gently, and with light. . . . It grieves for its offenses against God; yet, on the other hand, His mercy lifts its spirits. (K, 1: 197–198)

When Teresa is able to identify the despair of an overwhelming sense of worthlessness as false humility, true humility emerges as the right to accept God's love. I do not mean to claim that Teresa's theological concepts are created *ex nihilo*. Mystic writers of the day stressed the need for humility to be accompanied by confidence in the grace of God. Excessive remorse of conscience (*escrúpulos*) was recognized as an impediment to the practice of mental prayer and spiritual progress. Teresa's originality lies not in doctrinal content per se but rather in her transformation of doctrine into a vital solution to her personal anguish. With her metacommunicative feat Teresa has effectively restructured the myth of women as victims of the devil's seduction. Teresa's devil seduces, yes, not by appealing to women's vainglory and promising them power, not by "transforming himself into an angel of light," but by tricking them into despairing of their power and attractiveness to God.

The fact that Teresa wrote from obedience and that she developed conscious strategies to ensure the receptivity of her readers is not incompatible with the idea that her writing in some way served her inner needs. Under the most adverse and restrictive circumstances Teresa wrote prodigiously, in an attempt to find—or imagine—a compassionate and receptive reader; in an attempt to find a means of articulating, for herself, the conflict between authority and authenticity, guilt and self-acceptance. She thus elaborated a rhetorical strategy of persuasion—an externally directed rhetoric that defends as it acquiesces. But as an introspective dialectic her rhetoric of humility becomes a metacommunicative statement *about* the double bind, delineating its pardoxes and affirming the existence of a justifying order beyond the power of its field.

Chapter III

THE WAY OF PERFECTION AND THE RHETORIC OF IRONY

IF TERESA'S first book was written at the command of her confessors, her second book, *The Way of Perfection*, was composed at the request of the nuns of the convent of San José in Avila. Teresa had originally hoped that her nuns would be able to read *The Book of Her Life*, which contained a section on the four stages of prayer. But her current confessor, Domingo Báñez, was reluctant to allow the book's dissemination among a female audience. He did grant Teresa permission to write for the nuns "a few things about prayer."[1] The pragmatic situation for the new text is thus radically changed: in *The Book of Her Life* Teresa had written primarily for male superiors; in *The Way of Perfection* she was addressing principally female subordinates. If the double bind injunction of the confessional autobiography

This chapter is a revised and expanded version of my article "Teresa's 'Delicious' Diminutives: Pragmatics and Style in *Camino de perfección*," originally published in the *Journal of Hispanic Philology* 10 (1986): 211–227.

[1] Báñez wrote in his Approbation of *The Book of Her Life*, "I have decided that this book should not be shown to all and sundry, but only to men of learning and experience and Christian discretion" (from *The Complete Works of Saint Teresa of Jesus*, trans. E. Allison Peers, 3 vols. [London: Sheed and Ward, 1944–1946], 3: 336. The original is found in *Obras completas*, edición manual, ed. Efrén de la Madre de Dios and Otger Steggink [Madrid: Católica, 1962], p. 179; all citations to Teresa's works in Spanish are to this edition, which will be referred to hereafter as *Obras* 1962). In his testimony for her canonization, he confessed that he became angry with Teresa when he discovered that several copies of the *Life* had been made, because "it was not proper for women's writings to become public" (*Procesos de beatificación y canonización de Santa Teresa de Jesús*, ed. Silverio de Santa Teresa, vols. 18–20 of Biblioteca mística carmelitana [Burgos: Tipografía de "El Monte Carmelo," 1934–1935], 20: 10).

had required Teresa to elaborate a rhetoric to defend herself before men, *The Way of Perfection* required a rhetoric to teach and inspire women. But although Teresa's principal addressees were women subordinates, her work still had to win the approval of her confessor and other male advisors—she still needed to avoid the appearance of appropriating the male apostolic privilege. Teresa's solution to the problem of addressing two different audiences was to use an extremely informal in-group register—a woman's language—which, in effect, would constitute a different kind of speech act in accordance with her divergent audience. This low-register language could count as a disavowal of any homiletic presumption before her male audience; at the same time her verbal informality constituted a gesture of solidarity toward the beleaguered nuns of the early Carmelite reform.

THE TWO VERSIONS OF THE TEXT

The Way of Perfection is an ideal text for examining Teresa's style, since she revised it extensively. The first version of the text, conserved in an autograph manuscript in the library of the Escorial, was begun between 1562 and 1566, quite probably after the second version of *The Book of Her Life* in 1565. Although Teresa tried repeatedly to secure Báñez' authorization, he refused to approve a work in which Teresa had so obviously exceeded the limits originally proposed. As we shall see, Teresa subtly transformed a gloss on oral prayer into a mystical treatise. In the 1591 Canonization Proceedings Báñez denied ever having anything to do with the work.[2] It was in fact García de Toledo who carried out the role of censor, crossing out a number of passages, sometimes scoring entire pages. But some of

[2] Francisco Márquez Villanueva, "La vocación literaria de Santa Teresa," *Nueva revista de filología hispánica* 32 (1983): 355–374; quotation pp. 362–363, n. 22. Márquez observes that this incidence is an excellent example of Teresa's remarkable ability to adapt the concept of "writing out of obedience" to her own purposes (p. 362).

Teresa's daring assertions remained intact, including her argument for the inseparability of mental prayer and fervent oral prayer.

When Teresa recopied the original manuscript, sometime between 1566 and 1569, she did much more than omit censored passages—she reorganized chapters and headings and eliminated many imaginative comparisons, exclamations, references to her personal experiences, and caustic comments about anticontemplatives and the Inquisition. Other changes can only be described as stylistic. Although there is still controversy over the date of the second version, or Valladolid codex, it is obvious that Teresa already had in mind a wider audience than the twelve nuns of San José. Teresa, by her own admission, usually wrote rapidly and sometimes lacked the opportunity even to read over what she had written. If Valladolid was intended for the same twelve nuns of San José, why should Teresa have done more than eliminate the censored passages?[3]

As manuscript copies proliferated, Teresa planned an edition for publication based on the Valladolid version. In the third version—the Toledo codex—some revisions were apparently collaborative. Nevertheless, Teresa's intervention is evident in the marginal corrections to the copy that appear in her own hand. The Toledo version, published in Évora in 1583, reflects, according to Efrén de la Madre de Dios and Otger Steggink, "the way she wanted it to reach

---

[3] For discussions of the textual history and debate over dating the work see the facsimile edition of *Camino*-E, edited by Tomás de la Cruz (Rome: Tipografia poliglotta vaticana, 1965), 2: pp. 9*–168*, esp. pp. 15–30* and 95–103*; *Obras* 1962, p. 181; and Daniel Pablo Maroto, "Camino de Perfección," in *Introducción a la lectura de Santa Teresa*, ed. Alberto Barrientos et al. (Madrid: Editorial de espiritualidad, 1978), pp. 269–310. Tomás de la Cruz favors the date 1566 for the first revision—just a few months after García de Toledo returned the original to Teresa with his corrections. Efrén de la Madre de Dios, Otger Steggink, and Daniel de Pablo Maroto prefer the date of 1569, that is, after the founding of the convents of Medina del Campo, Malagón, Valladolid, and Duruelo.

the general public."[4] Teresa apparently adopted a more formal and less ironic tone because the different versions of the text correlated to a widening margin of distance between the author and her readers. The principal addressees of *E* are a group of intimate friends; those of *V* include the nuns in recently founded and projected reformed convents, and possibly more male readers; *T*, published posthumously, is addressed to the invisible public. It should be stressed that Teresa's basic strategy is unchanged—she continues to use a low-register, affiliative language as a means of accommodation to a dual audience. But the revisions of *The Way of Perfection* allow us to observe, with particular clarity, not only the degree to which Teresa's stylistic decisions were deliberate but also the extent to which style was, for Teresa, a pragmatic issue.

A DUAL AUDIENCE

Teresa's original Prologue most clearly shows her in the process of juggling the contradictory demands of her dual audience. The interwoven acts of assertion and self-abasement, *apologia* and confession, developed in *The Book of Her Life* are again elaborated here. Teresa is eager to disclaim any egotistical motive for writing but subtly alludes to areas of expertise and experience. She protests that she has only agreed to take up the pen since she has been *importuned* so earnestly by her nuns. She concedes that there is really no need for another book on prayer, since there are already many excellent books on the subject; she allows, however, that sometimes imperfect works are more pleas-

---

[4] *Obras* 1962, p. 181. Although the revisions of Toledo continue the same trend, because of its collaborative nature I will concentrate my stylistic study on a comparison between Escorial and Valladolid. I shall use from here on the conventional abbreviations for the three versions: *E* for Escorial, *V* for Valladolid, and *T* for Toledo. Both the Escorial and Valladolid codices are printed on the same page in *Obras* 1962. The Toledo codex can be found in volume 2 of *Obras completas*, nueva revisión del texto original con notas críticas, ed. Efrén de la Madre de Dios, Otilio de Niño Jesús, and Otger Steggink, 3 vols. (Madrid: Católica 1951–1959).

ing than perfect ones. In spite of her inadequacy as a writer God may help her "get things right," but if she fails her confessor will burn the book, and she will have at least succeeded in obeying the faithful servants of God. She confesses that she is unable to hide her own wretchedness, but this will thus serve as a warning to her nuns. In this catalogue of by now familiar defensive humility formulae one passage strikes the reader as particularly ironic: "[Y] este amor, junto con los años y espiriencia que tengo de algunos monesterios, podrá ser aproveche para atinar en cosas menudas más que los letrados que, por tener otras ocupaciones más importantes y ser varones fuertes, no hacen tanto caso de las cosas que en sí no parecen nada y a cosa tan flaca como somos las mujeres todo nos puede dañar" (*Camino*-E, p. 184) 'It may be that this love [for the nuns], together with my years and the experience I have in a number of convents, will make me more successful in writing about small matters than learned men. For since they are strong men and have other more important concerns, they do not pay as much attention to things which seem nothing but which can do a lot of harm to creatures as weak as we women are.'[5] These "small matters," as the text will make clear, are nothing less than the difficulties and temptations of the pursuit of spiritual perfection. Hers is a book by a "weak woman" and for "weak women," which addresses the special temptations they face within the cloisters. It does not merit, she implies, detailed scrutiny by male readers who have more important demands on their time. Teresa's rhetoric, in short, is ironic, since her words are meant to be interpreted differently by her different audiences. She implicitly solicits a close reading

[5] For this chapter I felt it necessary to supply my own translations in order to communicate the low-register quality of Teresa's writing. Francisco Márquez Villanueva was the first to call attention to the irony of this passage in "Santa Teresa y el linaje," in *Espiritualidad y literatura en el siglo XVI*, by Francisco Márquez Villanueva (Madrid: Alfaguara, 1968), pp. 139–205; quotation p. 193.

from her nuns but suggests a cursory reading for "learned men."

A momentary lapse from irony only reinforces the impression that Teresa's acts of verbal deference to male authority cannot always be taken at face value. In an impassioned defense of the spiritual rights of women Teresa argues that Christ did not hate women when he was on earth and in fact found in them more faith and as much love as men. Temporarily casting aside any concession to the sensibilities of her male readers, she protests women's unjust treatment by the "sons of Adam":

[Q]ue no hagamos cosa q valga nada por Vos en público, ni osemos ablar algunas verdades que lloramos en secreto, sino q no nos aviades de oyr petición tan justa; no lo creo yo, Señor, de vra bondad y justicia, q sois justo juez y no como los jueçes del mundo, q como son yjos de Adán, y, en fin, todos varones, no ay virtud de mujer q no tengan por sospecha. . . . Veo los tiempos de manera que no es razón desechar ánimos virtuosos y fuertes, anq sean de mujeres.

(*Camino*-E, p. 193, n. 1)

For we can do nothing in public that is of any use to You, nor do we dare speak of some of the truths we weep over in silence, fearing You may not hear our just prayer. I do not believe this, Lord, of your justice and goodness, for You are a righteous Judge and not like the judges of the world, who are sons of Adam, and, after all, men, so there is no virtue in a woman that they do not consider suspect. . . . I see that times are so bad that it is not right to reject virtuous and strong spirits, even if they be women.

That Teresa had second thoughts about her unaccustomed explicitness is suggested by the fact that these lines are heavily scored in the original manuscript, probably censored by her own hand.[6]

---

[6] Tomás de la Cruz notes that two different hands marked the passage; he surmises that the words were scored with a horizontal line by the

Teresa took other risks on doctrinal grounds, however. Perhaps reassured by the success of the founding of San José and the support of the Bishop of Avila, perhaps assuming that her text would remain in the secure hands of those sympathetic to the Carmelite reform, she attacked anticontemplatives on many fronts. She ridiculed the ignorance of confessors and all those who believed that when women practiced mental prayer they invited diabolical possession. Even her criticism of the Inquisition is thinly veiled. Alluding to the Index of 1559, which forbade the publication of all vernacular books on religious themes, Teresa wrote, with obvious sarcasm, "Haced bien, hijas, que no os quitarán el Paternóster y el Avemaría" (*Camino*-E, p. 251) 'Hold fast, daughters, for they cannot take from you the Our Father and Hail Mary.' García de Toledo was hardly insensitive to the implication of the passage and, in addition to crossing out the words, added in the margin, "It seems that she is reproaching the Inquisitors who prohibit books of prayer."[7] In a sense Teresa had taken her confessor's vague concession to write for the nuns "a few things about prayer" and stretched it to the limits of contemporary orthodoxy. Buried within a notebook of advice on convent life, with a gloss on the Lord's Prayer, the perceptive reader can find a preliminary guidebook to *mental* prayer and a defense of women's rights to choose the path of spiritual perfection.

Teresa not only wrote on the censored topic of mental prayer, she also dismissed as irrelevant the controversy surrounding the issue. She proposed that the nuns recite the *Pater Noster* vocally with all their hearts, concentrating on the fact that prayer is conversation with God. Sweeping aside ponderous theological debate, she argued simply: "Sí, que no está la falta para no ser oración mental en tener cerrada la boca; si hablando estoy enteramente viendo que

---

censor and blacked out heavily by Teresa. One of the lines has yet to be deciphered. See Tomás, *Camino*, "Introducción," 2: 74*–75*.

[7] Ibid., 2: 73* and 76*; also see 2: 73*–83* for other instances of doctrinal censorship.

hablo con Dios con más advertencia que en las palabras
que digo, junto está oración mental y vocal. Salvo si no os
dicen que estéis hablando con Dios y rezando el Avemaría,
y pensando en el mundo; aquí callo" (*Camino*-E, p. 252)
'Yes, well you know mental prayer has nothing to do with
whether or not you keep your mouth closed. If I am clearly
seeing that I am talking with God and paying more attention to Him than the words that I am saying, mental and
oral prayer are joined together. If people say you are
speaking with God by reciting the Avemaría while thinking of the world—well, words fail me.'

A RHETORIC FOR SOLIDARITY

Teresa was eager not only to transmit her knowledge of
mental prayer to the nuns but to promote the tranquility
they would need to practice contemplation. Her break
with the Incarnation had incurred considerable ill-will
among her Calced sisters, and *converso* support for her reform had also stirred up anti-*converso* resentment. The
twelve nuns of San José, in spite of the bishop's blessing,
were still "impure" troublemakers in the eyes of many citizens of Avila. Consequently, during these early days of
the reform Teresa was greatly concerned with avoiding
factionalism within the convent. She saw danger in intense individual friendships, reflected in terms of endear-
ment: "[Estas ternuras] no se usan en esta casa ni se han
de usar, tal como 'mi vida', 'mi alma', ni otras cosas de
éstas, que a las unas llaman uno y a las otras otro. Estas
palabras regaladas déjenlas para con el Señor. . . . Es muy
de mujeres, y no querría yo mis hermanas pareciesen en
nada sino varones fuertes" (*Camino*-E, p. 209) 'These en-
dearments are not used and should not be used in this
house: "my life" "my soul" and similar things people say
to one another. Leave these affectionate words for the
Lord. They are very effeminate, and I do not want my sisters to seem like that in any way but rather to be like
strong men.' Though the masculine was apparently the

only paradigm available to describe the virtues of impartial comraderie she wished to inculcate, the image of gender inversion ends on a comic note: "que si ellas hacen lo que es en sí, el Señor las hará tan varoniles que espanten a los hombres" (Camino-E, p. 209) 'If they do all that is in their power, the Lord will make them so manly that they will frighten men.' The apparent homage to male virtue is thus undercut by the suggestion that women, when they put their minds to it, can surpass their male counterparts in spiritual fortitude.

Teresa is also scornful of "honor," a preoccupation she saw as a smoke screen for the contemporary obsession with purity of blood. Teresa believed that in order for her reform to survive, class and caste distinctions had to be left outside the convent walls. "Points of honor" are referred to with derogatory diminutives and other dismissive turns of phrase: "bando, u deseo de ser más, u puntillos" (Camino-E, p. 209) 'factions, or desire for higher status, or silly points of honor.' She urged the harshest punishment for any nun who promoted factions by vaunting her own lineage or impugning another's: "Mire mucho la perlada, por amor de Dios, en atajar presto esto, y cuando no bastare con amor, sean graves castigos. Si una lo alborota, procuren se vaya a otro monesterio, que Dios las remediará con que la doten. Echen de sí esta pestilencia, corten como pudieren las ramas, y si no bastare, arranquen la raíz" (Camino-E, pp. 209-210) 'For the love of God, let the prioress be most careful not to let this occur. She must put a stop to it from the start, and if love is not enough, she must use heavy punishments. If one of the nuns is stirring up trouble, try to send her to another convent, for God will provide a dowry for her. Drive this pestilence out, cut off its branches as best you can, and if that is not enough, pull it out by the roots.' Elsewhere she treats the problem with a lighter touch: "[S]obre cuál era de mijor tierra, que no es otra cosa sino debatir si será para lodo buena u para adobes" (Camino-E, p. 267) 'Arguing over who is from a better part of the country is the same as debating whether the dirt is better for bricks or mud walls.' Behind the insistence on equality we can see her fear that factionalism, inflamed by racism, might well attract the attention of the Inquisition and crush the incipient reform. Throughout the text we are impressed with a sense of beleaguerment—a need to avoid dissent within and to close ranks against a common foe. The first version of her text especially is characterized by the complementary aims of promoting solidarity and discouraging divisive behavior.

I have argued that Teresa artfully addresses her discourse to an actual dual audience of confessor and nuns. To serve her aims of correcting and encouraging the nuns of San José she also manipulates her audience on an imaginative level, dividing her *female* readers into hypothetical confederates and victims. This fictional audience bifurcation represents another level of irony in her text and functions as an ingenious verbal weapon that allows Teresa to engage in criticism and promote affiliation simultaneously. Irony as a critical weapon requires little elaboration since this concept corresponds with traditional notions of irony as *antiphrasis*, or blaming with praise. But how irony promotes a sense of affiliation is less obvious. Audience bifurcation, as David Kaufer has observed, is the key to irony's affiliative success. First of all, by targeting an out-group for censure irony reinforces in-group cohesiveness. Secondly, the audience of "confederates" that successfully recovers the intended meaning enjoys a sense of superiority over the misled audience of "victims."[8] Irony also encourages sympathetic identification because the author and the confederate audience must share interpretive assumptions. As Wayne Booth has expressed it: "The author I infer behind the false words is my kind of man, because he enjoys playing with irony, because he assumes *my* capacity for

[8] David Kaufer has developed the idea of irony and audience bifurcation in "Irony and Rhetorical Strategy," *Philosophy and Rhetoric* 10 (1977): 90–110, and in "Irony and the Theory of Meaning," *Poetics Today* 4 (1983): 451–464.

dealing with it, and—more important—because he grants me a kind of wisdom; he assumes that he does not have to spell out the shared and secret truths on which my reconstruction is to be built."[9]

But a speaker can also be ironic at his or her own expense. The self-effacing rhetor, the descendant of Aristotle's *eiron*, disavows all laudatory qualities. This self-mockery or self-effacement, as a gesture of positive politeness, signals approachability. The *eiron* trusts at least part of the audience to recognize the inconsistency between her exaggeratedly humble self-assessment and the truth. To summarize, whether the object of censure is a fictional out-group or the speaker herself, irony can be used as a positive politeness stratagem, affirming an intimate, common ground.

In *The Way of Perfection* Teresa uses irony—with a variety of ironic victims—and then partially retreats from the strategy with her revisions, as her audience becomes larger and more distant. In general the first version stresses shared values and attitudes, as well as equality in social status between the writer and her audience. The text is, moreover, replete with utterances that assume the intimate readers' capacity or willingness to recover oblique meanings. The playful balance between egalitarianism and authority shifts toward the latter pole in the second version. A shared perspective is no longer taken for granted, as Teresa repeatedly makes explicit what was stated indirectly in the original version. In the revised text the strategies of positive politeness are toned down and in some cases abandoned.

Humility topics abound in Teresa's autobiography and, as discussed earlier, were used as a defensive tactic of deference to her male superiors. However, in the context of an intimate, female audience many more humility topics are ironic—they are simply not meant to be taken literally.

[9] Booth, *A Rhetoric of Irony* (Chicago: University of Chicago Press, 1974), p. 28.

Teresa expects that her audience of confederates will see the incompatibility between her self-abasement and her true character, *which they already know*. For example, Teresa jokingly writes, "[C]omo ya tengo escrito en otra parte y otros muchos que saben lo que escriven (que yo por cierto que no lo sé; Dios lo sabe)" (*Camino*-E, p. 229) 'As I have already written elsewhere, and many others who know what they're writing (because I certainly don't know, God knows).' Here the humility topic is not to be taken entirely at face value since its paranomastic repetition is a manifestation of the verbal art she denies in the same breath. In the following example Teresa pretends to hide but simultaneously confesses to a fault, enfolding the depreciatory remark in a witty *negatio*: "Parece que desatino; pues no hago, que mayores cosas que éstas hace el amor divino, y por no parecer curiosa—ya que lo soy—y daros mal ejemplo, no trayo aquí algunas" (*Camino*-E, p. 231) 'It seems I'm talking nonsense; but I'm not, for divine love has done greater things than these, and since I don't want to seem overly picky—since I am—and be a bad example for you, I'm not going to give any examples.' These passages are eliminated in *V*, as are many other examples of self-depreciation. This tendency to use self-depreciation to diminish hierarchical difference is especially clear in the following remark: "Y ansí no sé para qué lo digo, pues, en parte, todas las que ahora aquí estáis me podéis en esto enseñar a mí; que confieso en este caso tan importante soy la más imperfecta; mas, pues me lo mandáis, tocaré en algunas cosas que se me ofrecen" (p. 210) 'And so I don't know why I'm saying this, since, in part, all of you who are here now could teach me; for I confess that in this very important matter I am the most imperfect, but since you command me, I will touch on some points.' But in *V*, although the audience-flattering assertion "you could teach me" remains, the humility stance is toned down to "in this important matter I am not as perfect as I would wish."

In sum, Teresa's self-depreciating remarks in *The Way of Perfection* are frequently hyperbolically ironic: what is said is an exaggerated form of what is meant. When she addressed the nuns of San José, Teresa assumed these remarks would be understood as verbal gestures of solidarity and not as a literal statement. When Teresa tones down or eliminates self-depreciating remarks in *V*, she does so not because she has become less humble in the intervening period but because she is less certain of her audience's ability to perceive the incompatibility between her literal and implied meaning.

Teresa's ironic hyperboles are not directed solely at herself; she sets up hypothetical nuns for ridicule in a way that allows her to chasten her addressees without chastising them directly.[10] For example, in *E* she describes nuns who do penance only sporadically as follows: "[A]lgunas veces dales un frenesí de hacer penitencias sin camino ni concierto, que duran dos días" (p. 215) 'Sometimes without rhyme or reason they go into a frenzy to do penances that last two days.' In *V*, *frenesí* ("frenzy") is modulated to *deseo* ("desire"). Nuns who complain loudly over minor ailments are similarly derided: "Cosa imperfectísima me parece, hermanas mías, este aullar y quejar siempre y enflaquecer la habla haciéndola de enferma" (p. 216) 'My sisters, this howling and constant complaining and whimpering to appear sick seems to me to be a very grave defect.' The triple-infinitive phrase, with its humorous exaggeration, in *V* becomes simply "este quejarnos siempre con livianos males" 'this constant complaining about slight discomfort.' Exaggeration and an inclusive "we" is used as a critical weapon when she refers to "unos malecillos que se pueden pasar en pie sin que matemos a todos con ellos" (*E*, p. 217) 'slight indisposition that can be en-

---

[10] Even when the addressee is unsure of her status as victim or confederate, ironic attacks could arguably emphasize common ground: anthropologists have observed that mock hostility (teasing and joking) is a universal sign of intimacy (Penelope Brown and Stephen Levinson, "Universals in Language Usage: Politeness Phenomena," in *Questions and Politeness: Strategies in Social Interaction*, ed. Esther Goody [Cambridge: At the University Press, 1978], pp. 56–289 at p. 129).

dured on foot without having us killing ourselves.' This flippant hyperbole is also omitted in *V*. Again, I doubt that Teresa had become more tolerant of malingering nuns when she revised her original text. Rather, for the wider audience in-group humor had to be toned down.

Another ironic device related to audience bifurcation is the use of *oratio recta* or direct discourse. In her original text Teresa on occasion mockingly echoes, as if in direct discourse, opinions that she implicitly rejects.[11] In the following citation she ironically repeats the opinion that nuns should be restricted to one confessor: "Si las tristes piden otro [confesor], luego va todo perdido el concierto de la relisión; u que si no es de su Orden, aunque fuese un san Jerónimo, luego hacen afrenta de la Orden toda" (*E*, p. 201) 'If the poor things ask for another confessor, then the harmony of the convent is completely lost, and if he's from another order, unless he's a Saint Jerome, then they're insulting the entire order.' In *V* the humorous exaggeration (*las tristes, todo, san Jerónimo, toda*; the poor things, completely, Saint Jerome, entire), along with the pretense at direct discourse, is eliminated. The shift to *indirect* discourse is emphasized by the repetition of *parece*: "Si piden otro, luego *parece* va perdido el concierto de la relisión; u que si no es de la Orden, aunque sea un santo, aun tratar con él les *parece* les hace afrenta" 'If they ask for another confessor, then *it seems* as if the harmony of the convent is lost, and if he's not from the order, *it seems* as if he's insulting them' (my emphasis).

The following passage from *E* has a similar sardonic tone: "Pues guardaos, hijas, de unas humildades que pone el demonio con gran inquietud de la gravedad de pecados pasados: 'si merezco llegarme al Sacramento', 'si me

---

[11] For a more detailed discussion of this type of irony, see Dan Sperber and Deirdre Wilson, "Irony and the Use-Mention Distinction," in *Radical Pragmatics*, ed. Peter Cole (New York: Academic Press, 1981), pp. 295–318. Brown and Levinson also note "point of view operations" or "deixis manipulation" as a positive politeness tactic. By using directly quoted speech, they argue, the speaker indicates that he shares the hearer's point of view ("Universals," pp. 123–124, 127).

dispuse bien', 'que no soy para vivir entre buenos' " (p. 308) 'Be careful, daughters, of a seeming humility that the devil puts us up to, a great uneasiness about the seriousness of past sins: "Do I deserve to approach the Sacrament," "Did I prepare myself well," "I'm not fit to live with good people."' Again, *V* eliminates the playful appropriation of a fictional out-group voice. Teresa begins with the same advice about "seeming humility" but then drops the pretense of first-person *oratio recta* for an impersonal "they": "Que suele apretar aquí de muchas maneras, hasta apartarse de las comuniones y de tener oración particular (por no lo merecer, les pone el demonio), y cuando llegan a el Santísimo Sacramento, en si se aparajaron bien u no" 'For he [the devil] generally presses hard on this point in different ways, until they are tempted to stay away from Communion and have private prayer (for the devil makes them feel they don't deserve it), and when they approach the Holy Sacrament, they wonder whether they have prepared well or not.' Nuns who fail to attend choir are ridiculed with absurd exaggeration of their complaints in direct discourse: "[D]ejamos de ir al coro . . . un día porque nos dolió [la cabeza] y otro porque nos ha dolido, y otros tres porque no nos duela" (*E*, p. 215) 'We stop going to choir one day because we have a headache, another day because we had a headache, and for the next three because we don't have a headache.' The second version dispenses with the mocking repetitiveness and states simply: "Y a las veces es poco el mal, y nos parece no estamos obligadas a hacer nada" 'Sometimes the illness is slight, and it seems that we aren't required to do anything.' Although *V* retains the inclusive "we," Teresa is much more careful to differentiate her own opinions from the ones she is ridiculing.

"Delicious" Diminutives

An obvious feature of Teresa's familiar, in-group language is her abundant use of diminutives. Traditionally Teresa's diminutives have been seen as a manifestation of her spontaneous, "affective femininity." "Teresa uses the precise, loving diminutive to tinge her entire thought with the most delicious femininity," wrote Rafael Lapesa in his history of the language. [12] And E. A. Peers argued, "The two concomitants of familiar Spanish conversation—especially among women—are an excess of diminutives and a continual—frequently an effective—recourse to the superlative. Both diminutives and superlatives abound in St. Teresa"; "We have proof, both of the naturalness with which she wrote of mystical experiences and of the extent to which diminutive-making was a habit with her."[13] Menéndez Pidal believed that Teresa felt an "irrepressible attraction" toward this grammatical form.[14]

There is certainly a widespread notion that Spanish diminutives are feminine—or effeminate—as well as a long-standing prejudice that diminutives belong to low-register, nonpublic and familiar language.[15] As early as 1580

---

[12] Lapesa, *Historia de la lengua española*, 9th ed. (Madrid: Gredos, 1984), p. 318. Emilio Náñez Fernández (*El diminutivo: Historia y funciones en el español clásico y moderno* [Madrid: Gredos, 1973], p. 192) expresses a similar judgment. More recently Mary Cleopha Cipar has written, "In Teresa's works, the intimate quality of colloquial expression is heightened by delicate diminutives which clothe ordinary words with feminine charm and tenderness" ("The Portrait of Teresa of Avila as Woman and as Saint in *Camino de perfección*," [Ph.D. diss., University of Pittsburgh, 1983], p. 93).

[13] Peers, *Studies of the Spanish Mystics*, 2d ed. (London: Macmillan, 1951–), 1: 176; Peers, "Saint Teresa's Style: A Tentative Appraisal," in *Saint Teresa of Jesus and Other Essays and Addresses* (London: Faber and Faber, 1953), p. 87.

[14] Ramón Menéndez Pidal, "El estilo de Santa Teresa," in *La lengua de Cristóbal Colón y otros estudios sobre el Siglo XVI*, by Ramón Menéndez Pidal (Madrid: Espasa Calpe, 1958), pp. 119–142; quotation pp. 126–127.

[15] See, for example, Clemente Hernando Balmori, "Habla mujeril," *Filología* 8 (1962): 123–138 at p. 133; Alberto Zuloaga Ospina, "La función del diminutivo en español," *Thesaurus* 25 (1970): 23–48 at p. 38 and p. 47; José Joaquín Montes Giraldo, "Funciones del diminutivo en español: Ensayo de clasificación," *Thesaurus* 27 (1972): 71–88 at p. 87; and Amado Alonso, "Noción, emoción, acción y fantasía en los diminutivos," in *Estudios lingüísticos: Temas españoles* by Amado Alonso (Madrid: Gredos, 1951), pp. 193–299 quotation p. 216.

Better Homes and Gardens
CRAFTS CLUB
®

PO BOX 10646
DES MOINES IOWA 50336-0646

Better Homes and Gardens®

CRAFTS CLUB

P.O. Box 10646
Des Moines, Iowa 50336-0646

You now have **00** Bonus Credits.

☐ Send me the Editors' Choice Immediately
☐ In addition to or ☐ Instead of Editors' Choice send me:

Order #	Title
2800	HOLLY QUILT X-STITCH
2709	COUNTRY CLASSICS:25 PROJ
2837	INNOVATIVE SEWING
2734	QUICK THICK MACHINE KNIT
2702	WEDDING FLOWERS

☐☐☐☐☐☐☐☐☐☐

☑ Send me nothing this month.

▶ **Account Number** ▶

C70939707   23121015

L HIRSCHLER
14471 COUNTY RD 48
SYRACUSE IN 46567

C70939707   C70939707   01RG   37

Editors' Choice
2906 SCRAP SAV/CRCHT SWTR

MUST BE RECEIVED BY ▶ JUN 12, 1991
To assure timely receipt, mail at least 7 DAYS before this date

Please make any address changes above

Fernando de Herrera wrote that diminutives make a language feminine, lascivious, and frivolous, and this idea was repeated in subsequent grammars.[16] But although the perception that "diminutives are feminine" may be difficult or impossible to prove empirically, such "folklinguistic" notions can, as Deborah Cameron has argued, exert an influence on the linguistic choices individuals make.[17] If a certain feature is perceived as "low register" or "feminine," it would be avoided in circumstances that would favor "high-register" or "masculine" language.

It is quite conceivable that Teresa was aware of the prejudice against diminutives in formal discourse and nonetheless used them intentionally as a way of disavowing the public, didactic status of her language. Furthermore, the fact that of the sixty-eight diminutives in *E* Teresa eliminated twenty-six, or nearly a third, in *V* seems to argue persuasively that their high frequency in this text was a deliberate stylistic choice and *not* the result of a spontaneous or irrepressible outpouring of feminine affectivity.[18]

But even if Teresa used diminutives abundantly to mark her text as "feminine," or more specifically low-register, nonthreatening discourse, there is nothing that is particularly delicate or affectionate about their connotations. The semantic range of diminutives is notoriously wide: they

[16] *Obras de Garci Lasso de la Vega con anotaciones de Fernando de Herrera,* 2d ed. facsimilar de Antonio Gallego Morell (Madrid: Centro Superior de Investigaciones Científicas, 1973), p. 554, cited by Náñez, *El diminutivo,* p. 59. The same idea is repeated, almost verbatim, by Antonio de Capamny y de Montpalau in his 1812 *Filosofía de la elocuencia,* cited by Náñez, *El diminutivo,* p. 72.

[17] Cameron, *Feminism and Linguistic Theory,* (London: Macmillan, 1985), pp. 31–34. For a study of gender and diminutives in Dutch see Dédé Brouwer, "The Influence of the Addressee's Sex on Politeness in Language Use," *Linguistics* 20 (1982): 697–711. Brouwer's results do not support the "folk-linguistic" notion that women use more diminutives than men. Instead, she found a greater correlation between age of speaker and diminutive usage: specifically, in a controlled speech setting young men and women used more diminutives than their elders.

[18] For a more detailed quantitative analysis of diminutive revisions see Weber, "Teresa's 'Delicious' Diminutives."

can connote disdain, belittlement, condescension, disgust, irony, sarcasm, euphemism, modesty, as well as affection and small size.[19] In *The Way of Perfection* Teresa's language exploits the diminutive's hard-hitting pejorative, obliquely ironic, as well as affectionate connotations. Furthermore, when she revised the text in a way that is consistent with the revisions discussed above, she censored primarily those diminutives that were used ironically and pejoratively.

We find, for example, ironic self-depreciation in: "¿No es linda cosa una pobre monjita de san José que pueda llegar a señorear toda la tierra y elementos?" (*E*, p. 241) 'Isn't it something that a poor little nun from San José should come to lord it over the earth and the elements?' *V* reduces *monjita* to *monja*. Similarly, "[A]proveche este aviso de esta pecadorcilla de despertador" 'May the advice from this poor little sinner be useful to you as a reminder' in *V* becomes "[A]proveche esto que me havéis mandado escrivir por despertador" 'May this which you have ordered me to write be useful as a reminder' (p. 188). "Vamos a otras cosillas" 'let's go on to some other little matters' is changed to a more authoritative "Vamos a otras cosas" 'Let's go on to other matters' in *V* (p. 218). Teresa also eliminates the self-depreciatory "*consideracioncita*" from "Allegada a este Maestro de toda la sabiduría, quizá me enseñará alguna consideracioncita que os contente" (*E*, p. 249) 'Having grown close to his Master of all wisdom, perhaps He'll teach me some little thought that will please you.' A mock insult directed at the "dull" reader is also dropped, so that "digo el cuerpo, que alguna simplecita verná que no sepa qué es interior y esterior" (*E*, p. 278) 'I say the body, be-

---

[19] A historical survey on the evolution of diminutives can be found in Náñez, *El diminutivo*. He lists semantic variations on p. 380. For tendencies in semantic/suffix correlation in modern Spanish consult Anthony Gooch, *Diminutive, Augmentative and Pejorative Suffixes in Modern Spanish*, 2d ed. (Oxford: Pergamon, 1970). Amado Alonso's highly influential study ("Noción") was the first to suggest the pragmatic function of diminutives.

cause some silly little fool will come along who doesn't know what's interior and exterior' becomes in V "digo el cuerpo, porque mijor me entendáis" 'I say the body so that you may understand me better.' The obviously sardonic "Bonico es el mundo para gustar dél quien ha comenzado a gozar de Dios" 'It's a fine world for one to enjoy who has started to enjoy God' is softened in V: "No deve ser con contento quien ha comenzado a gozar" (p. 318) 'It must not be pleasant to live in the world once one has started to enjoy God.' The equally sarcastic exclamation "¡Válame Dios, tocar en un puntito de honra!" (E, p. 232) 'God help me, worrying about a little point of honor' is eliminated entirely in the revised text.

In the following diminutive, also reduced in V, irony works through understatement: "[M]e parece que esto de honra siempre trai algún interesillo de tener rentas y dineros" (E, p. 188) 'It seems to me that this matter of honor always brings with it a slight interest in having income and money.' A major theme of Camino is Teresa's insistent desire to found an unendowed convent, precisely to avoid class distinctions and to free nuns from the obligations to powerful patrons.[20] Therefore interesillo is ironically understated, since for Teresa interés was not a slight but a major threat to the spiritual autonomy of her reformed convents.

In a similar manner Teresa contrasts the mutual affection of contemplatives with the profane attachments of ordinary men and women as follows: "[M]erece nombre de amor, no estos amorcitos desastrados valadíes de por acá (E, p. 206)" 'This deserves the name of love, and not the dirty, trivial little loves down here.' "Amorcitos" is indeed depreciatory, but Teresa's repugnance toward this kind of "love" is ironically understated. She rejects all possible ambiguity in V: "Esta es voluntad, y no estos quereres de por acá desastrados" 'This is love, and not these dirty desires down here.'

The meiotic irony of some of the diminutives is very

[20] This topic is treated more fully in Chapter V.

subtle. Teresa writes, "¿Qué esposa hay que, recibiendo muchas joyas de valor de su esposo, no le dé siquiera una sortijica . . . ?" (p. 256) 'What wife, having received many valuable jewels from her husband, wouldn't give him even one insignificant little ring?' The depreciatory "sortijica" 'insignificant ring' is the term of comparison for nothing less than constancy in the practice of mental prayer, as the continuation of the passage makes clear: "Pues ¿qué menos merece este Señor para que burlemos de él, dando y tomando una nonada que le damos?" 'Then how much less does our Lord deserve for us to tease him, giving and taking back the little nothing that we give him?' The effort of mental prayer, Teresa implies, is insignificant *in comparison* with God's gifts. Not trusting her wider audience to take the depreciation with a grain of salt, Teresa changes "*sortijica*" to "*sortija*" in *V*.

WRITING LIKE A WOMAN

We can see then that just as Teresa toned down other manifestations of irony in *V*, she tended to eliminate the diminutives that were ironically hyperbolic, sardonic, or meiotic. The affectionate diminutives, on the other hand, survived intact for the most part.[21] Teresa's revisions reflect the tendency observable throughout the second version to produce a more formal text by reducing its irony— by eliminating or toning down hyperbole, sarcasm, understatement, and mocking *oratio recta*. The verbal obliqueness that implies mutual interpretive strategies is attenuated, though not entirely replaced, with a more authoritative directness.

The assertion that Teresa "wrote like a woman" needs to be made with numerous qualifications. We can no longer accept notions of a "deliciously" feminine style, that is, the assumption that her linguistic patterns reflect

[21] Five additional depreciatory or pejorative diminutives are eliminated from *T*, whereas only one affectionate diminutive is changed.

an innate feminine mystique. Teresa consciously adopted, as a rhetorical strategy, linguistic features that were associated with women, in the sense that women's discourse coincided with the realm of low-prestige, nonpublic discourse. Teresa's feminine rhetoric was affiliative, but this does not mean that it was especially tender or delicate. Rather, by selectively adapting features from the language of subordinate groups, Teresa hoped to create a subversive discourse that was at once public and private, didactic and supportive, authoritative and familiar. Her strategy was of necessity duplicitous. Teresa's rhetoric for women was an ironic rhetoric, used, first of all, to gain access to her audience and, secondly, to reinforce the bonds of a small interpretive community. As that community grew, Teresa proved that she was capable of modulating her strategy and her ironically feminine style.

Chapter IV

THE INTERIOR CASTLE AND THE RHETORIC OF OBFUSCATION

LAS MORADAS del castillo interior or The Interior Castle has often been considered Teresa's masterpiece, her most systematic presentation of the mystical experience, expounded with her most delicate figurative language. Yet, although an allegory, its coherence is elusive, for there is no one-to-one correspondence between literal signifier and allegorical signified. The soul as castle, the Christian as warrior and pilgrim, salvation as a city, man as microcosmos, Christ as bridegroom—all of these motifs contributed to the creation of Teresa's interior castle, but no one strand dominates all the rest.[1] Even the spatial disposition

[1] Source studies have shown that Teresa drew upon her wide readings in secular and religious literature including the chivalric novel, medical treatises, and the Scriptures. The most immediate sources appear to be Francisco de Osuna and Bernardino de Laredo (Robert Ricard, "Le symbolisme du Chateau Intérieur chez Sainte Thérèse," Bulletin hispanique 67 [1965]: 25–41 at 26–30). Joseph Chorpenning has seen a connection between the image of the castle and the ideal of monastic life as militia spiritualis ("The Monastery, Paradise and the Castle: Literary Images and Spiritual Development in St. Teresa of Avila," Bulletin of Hispanic Studies 62 [1985]: 245–257); Javier Herrero points out the influence of chivalric romance ("The Knight and the Mystical Castle," Studies in Formative Spirituality 4 [1983]: 393–407); and Francisco Márquez Villanueva and Aurora Egido have noted the motif of man as microcosmos, waging a battle in the body (Márquez Villanueva, "El símil del castillo interior: Sentido y génesis," in Congreso internacional Teresiano 4–7 octubre, 1982, ed. Teófanes Eigdo Martínez et al. [Salamanca: Universidad de Salamanca, 1983], 2: 495–522; Aurora Egido, "La configuración alegórica de El castillo interior," Boletín del Museo e Instituto Camón Aznar 10 [1983]: 69–93. Aurora Egido provides the most exhaustive study to date on the sources. Cabalistic and Sufi sources are discussed by Catherine Swietlicki, Spanish Christian Ca-

of the castle is elusive; attempts by Teresa's exegetes to produce a pictorial representation of its seven dwelling places have proved curiously inconsistent. Although its inconsistencies may reflect Teresa's frustration with the inevitable tension between systematized theology and affective spirituality,[2] they are also a response to external sources of pressure. As usual, Teresa made a virtue out of necessity, resisted the unity allegory demanded, and actually emphasized the improvisational nature of her writing in a way that made it possible for her to take greater risks in terms of its doctrine. A Bride is hidden in Teresa's castle: the dangerous language of erotic spirituality is concealed by a proliferation of competing images. Her avowed incompetence constitutes in reality a rhetoric of obfuscation.

This is not to say that the improvisational quality was entirely rhetorical. *The Interior Castle* was written in 1577, during a particularly difficult period in Teresa's life. The Seville foundation had provoked even greater local hostility than usual. María del Corro, a disgruntled nun, denounced the prioress, Teresa, and her confessor Gracián to the Inquisition, accusing them of immoral conduct and Illuminism. Although the Inquisition dismissed the case, Teresa underwent rigorous examination. As we shall see in the next chapter, two other nuns in Seville began to report visions and revelations that alarmed Teresa. At the same time, in the acrimonious struggle between Calced and Discalced the latter were rapidly losing ground. Rubeo, the Carmelite superior general, turned against Teresa's reform, forbade further foundations, and ordered her reclusion in the Toledo convent. Teresa's beloved John of the Cross spent months of 1577 in a Calced jail in Toledo. Nicolás Ormaneto, papal nuncio and supporter of the Dis-

bala: *The Works of Luis de León, Santa Teresa de Jesús, and San Juan de la Cruz* (Columbia: University of Missouri Press, 1986), pp. 43–81.

[2] This is the theory proposed by Joseph Chorpenning, "The Literary and Theological Method of *The Interior Castle*," *Journal of Hispanic Philology* 3 (1979): 121–133 at 130.

calced, died in the same year, shortly after Teresa began work on *The Interior Castle*. His successor, Felipe Sega, was the very official who would characterize Teresa as a restless gadabout. Factional struggles at the Avila convent forced Teresa to interrupt her writing for almost five months. She also suffered poorer health than usual at this time and complained of headaches, nausea, and a "great noise" in her ears.[3] For these reasons it is likely that *The Interior Castle* underwent fewer revisions than *The Book of Her Life* or *The Way of Perfection*. Although Teresa was probably exaggerating when she protested that she hadn't had time to reread what she had written, it is also plausible that in this difficult year the pressures on her time and composure must have been particularly intense.

WOMEN'S LANGUAGE, WOMEN'S CHATTER

As in *The Way of Perfection* Teresa presents her writing both as an act of obedience to her confessor, Gracián, and as an act of compliance to her spiritual sisters, who have requested clarifications on certain aspects of mental prayer:

> Díjome quien me mandó escrivir que, como estas monjas de estos monesterios de nuestra Señora del Carmen tienen necesidad de quien algunas dudas de oración las declare y que le parecía que *mijor se entienden el lenguage unas mujeres de otras*, y con el amor que me tienen les haría más al caso lo que les dijese, tiene entendido por esta causa será de alguna importancia si se acierta a decir alguna cosa, y por esto iré hablando con ellas en lo que escriviré.
>
> Y porque parece desatino pensar que puede hacer al caso a otras personas, harta merced me hará nuestro Señor si a

---

[3] For the Seville denunciations see Enrique Llamas-Martínez, *Santa Teresa de Jesús y la Inquisición española* (Madrid: Centro Superior de Investigaciones Científicas, 1972), pp. 62–92; for the conflicts within the Carmelite order see Efrén de la Madre de Dios and Otger Steggink, *Tiempo y vida de Santa Teresa*, 2d rev. ed. (Madrid: Católica, 1977), pp. 701–805.

alguna de ellas se aprovechare para alabarle algún poquito
más. Bien sabe Su Majestad que yo no pretendo otra cosa.[4]

The one who ordered me to write told me that the nuns in
these monasteries of our Lady of Mount Carmel need someone to answer their questions about prayer and that he
thought *they would better understand the language used between
women*, and that because of the love they bore me they
would pay more attention to what I would tell them. I thus
understood that it was important for me to manage to say
something. So, I shall be speaking to them while I write; it's
nonsense to think that what I say could matter to other persons. Our Lord will be granting me favor enough if some of
these nuns benefit by praising Him a little more. His Majesty
well knows that I don't aim for anything else.[5]

Teresa, with Gracián's urging, can thus claim and defend
the writer's privilege in undeniably pragmatic terms: she,
as a woman, can reach a female audience because they
share a "language" and are bound by affectionate ties. Teresa not only explicitly claims to be using a "women's language," she also identifies it as an oral language: "So, I
shall be speaking to them while I write."
Teresa accordingly treats her readers as listeners, creat-
ing the impression that her remarks are part of an impro-
vised conversation. She seems to visualize the nuns' presence, "reading" their responses on their faces: "Paréceme
que aun no os veo satisfechas" (5:1:374)[6] 'It seems to me
that you're still not satisfied'; "Paréceme que estáis con deseo de ver qué se hace esta palomica" (5:4:382) 'It seems to

---

[4] *Las moradas del castillo interior*, in *Obras completas*, edición manual, ed.
Efrén de la Madre de Dios and Otger Steggink, (Madrid: Católica, 1962),
Prólogo, p. 345. All other Spanish citations to Teresa's works in this chap-
ter follow this edition, hereafter abbreviated as *Obras* 1962.

[5] Translations for *Las moradas del castillo interior* are by Kieran Kavanaugh and Otilio Rodríquez, *The Interior Castle* (New York: Paulist Press,
1979), p. 34, my emphasis; hereafter abbreviated as K.

[6] For the convenience of those who wish to consult other Spanish editions my citations will refer to the *morada*, the chapter, and then the page
from *Obras* 1962, with each division separated by a colon.

me you have a desire to see what this little dove is doing
. . .' (K, p. 102); "Paréceme que os estoy mirando cómo
decís . . ." (6:6:402) 'It seems to me I can see you asking
. . .' (K, p. 140). She also articulates their side of the dia-
logue: "Pues diréisme . . ." (6:4:395) 'Well now you will
ask me . . .' (K, p. 128); "Diréis que, si no se ve, que cómo
se entiende que es Cristo" (6:8:409) 'You will ask how if
nothing is seen one knows that it is Christ' (K, p. 153).

Margit Frenk has recently called attention to the way in
which such binomial pairs as "hear and read," "listeners
and readers," and "write and say" occur as near syno-
nyms in some Renaissance texts, and proposes that the
medieval practice of oral, collective reading complemented
the more modern practice of silent reading well into the
seventeenth century.[7] Convent life offered then (and still
does today) many opportunities for communal readings,
as nuns gather for meals, work, or recreation. Thus, the
flavor of the colloquial, especially notable in *The Interior
Castle*, may reflect the actual way in which Teresa's written
works were initially transmitted.[8] But compared with contemporary works, both recreational and devotional, Teresa's insistent evocation of "readers/listeners" occurs with
a totally new distribution and frequency that suggests other
pragmatic motives. First of all, Teresa's text, as we shall
see, is often allusive, especially in the later chapters. To
achieve her pedagogical goals in dangerous times Teresa
may have counted on an oral complement to the written
word. Conceivably, an allusive text could have been used

---

[7] Frenk, " 'Lectores y oidores': La difusión oral de la literatura en el
siglo de oro," in *Actas del séptimo congreso de la Asociación Internacional de
Hispanistas*, ed. Giuseppe Bellini (Rome: Bulzone, 1982), 1: 101–123, and
"Ver, oír, leer . . ." in *Homenaje a Ana María Barrenechea*, ed. Lía Schwartz
Lerner and Isaías Lerner (Madrid: Castalia, 1984), pp. 235–240.

[8] Angel Raimundo Fernández also notes the "presence" of the nuns in
Teresa's discourse and surmises that the book may have been intended
for communal oral readings ("Génesis y estructura de *Las moradas*," in
Congreso internacional Teresiano 4–7 octubre, 1982, ed. Teófanes Eigdo Martínez et al. [Salamanca: Universidad de Salamanca, 1983], 2: 609–636;
quotation p. 614).

as a mnemonic "backup" or stimulus for an oral transmission of knowledge.[9] Secondly, Teresa's insistence on the colloquial places a woman's text within the protective confines of women's conversation. She disavows its authority as *text*, denying both textual precedents and textual transmission.

The depreciatory statements about women in this work must be understood as part of a strategy that carves out an area of "insignificant" discourse unworthy of male scrutiny. "No sería tiempo perdido, hermanas, el que gastásedes en leer esto ni yo en escrivirlo, si quedásemos con estas dos cosas que los letrados y entendidos muy bien las saben; mas nuestra torpeza de las mujeres todo lo ha menester, y ansí por ventura quiere el Señor que vengan a nuestra noticia semejantes comparaciones" (1:2:349) 'The time you spend in reading this, or I in writing it, Sisters, would not be lost if we were left with these two blessings. Learned and wise men know about these things very well, but everything is necessary for our womanly dullness of mind; and so perhaps the Lord wills that we get to know comparisons like these' (K, p. 41). When she returns to the text after the five months' interruption, she complains that she doesn't have the time to reread and revise and may therefore repeat some of what she has said before, but she excuses herself as follows: "Como es para mis hermanas, poco va en ello" (5:4:382) 'Since this work is for my Sisters, the disorder won't matter much' (K, p. 103).

The ironic humor observed in *The Way of Perfection* reappears in this text and contributes to the colloquial tone. With *oratio recta* Teresa mocks spiritually timid nuns: "Dios nos libre . . . de pusilaminidad [sic] y corvadía, de mirar si me miran, no me miran, si yendo por este camino me sucederá mal, si osaré comenzar aquella obra, si será sobervia, si es bien que una persona tan miserable trate de cosa

[9] For the relationship between this text and contemporary mnemonic techniques see Michael Gerli, "El castillo interior y el Arte de la memoria," in Santa Teresa y la literatura mística hispánica, ed. Manuel Criado de Val (Madrid: EDI–6, 1984), pp. 331–337.

tan alta como la oración" (1:2:350–351) 'God deliver us
from cowardice, from "What if they're looking at me" and
"What if something bad happens to me on this path" and
"Do I dare do such a deed" and "Is it really good for someone as bad as me to engage in something as lofty as
prayer" ' (my translation). "Weepy" nuns are derided
with a broadly colloquial turn of phrase: ". . . que no parece han de acabar de llorar; y como ya tienen entendido
que las lágrimas son buenas, no se van a la mano ni quer-
rían hacer otra cosa" (6:6:402) '. . . for it seems they will
never leave off crying. Since they have already gotten the
idea that tears are good, they go too heavy on it and won't
do anything else' (my translation). The depreciatory diminutive is used with great effectiveness in this context:
". . . unas personas tiernas, que por cada cosita lloran"
(6:6:402) '. . . tender persons, who weep over every little
thing' (K, p. 140). Teresa's humor occasionally takes the
form of a sardonic question "Pensáis que es poca turbación
estar una persona muy en su sentido y verse arrebatar el
alma?" (6:5:398) 'Do you think it is a small disturbance for
a person to be very much in his senses and see his soul
carried off?' (K, p. 133). Although this inclusive irony is
not used nearly as much as it is in *The Way of Perfection*, it
functions similarly as an expression of informal solidarity.
The explicit readers, the nuns, are consulted, advised, flat-
tered but also teased in a way that underscores the in-
group, nonpublic nature of the discourse.

THE RHETORIC OF INCOMPETENCE

As a complementary tactic Teresa frequently calls attention
to her incompetence, and in this text, which is based on
an extended analogy, she in particular seems to point out
her dissatisfaction with her *"comparaciones"* or similes. She
protests that language, even with the help of comparisons,
is inadequate for describing the fifth dwelling place: "Creo
fuera mejor no decir nada de las que faltan, pues no se ha
de saber decir ni el entendimiento lo sabe entender ni las

comparaciones pueden servir de declararlo" (5:1:373) 'I believe it would be better not to say anything about these remaining rooms, for there is no way of learning how to speak of them; neither is the intellect capable of understanding them nor can comparisons help in explaining them' (K, p. 85). The favors of the sixth *morada* are so delicate that she knows no comparison "will fit": "[N]o sé comparación que poner que caudre" (6:2:388). After comparing the soul in rapture to a drunkard, Teresa acknowledges, "Harto groseras comparaciones son éstas para tan preciosa causa, mas no alcanza otras mi ingenio" (6:6:403) 'These are [coarse] comparisons for something so precious, but I can't think up any others' (K, p. 143). The writer herself is amused by the unusual similes and expects her readers will be as well: "Riéndome estoy de estas comparaciones, que no me contentan; mas no sé otras" (7:2:424) 'I am laughing to myself over these comparisons for they do not satisfy me, but I don't know any others' (K, p. 182). At other times she must make do with unsatisfactory similes: "Deseando estoy acertar a poner una comparación, para si pudiese dar a entender algo de esto que voy diciendo, y creo no la hay que caudre. Mas digamos ésta" (6:4:396) 'I have been wanting to find some comparison by which to explain what I'm speaking about, and I don't think there is any that fits. But let's use this one' (K, p. 129) At one point she rejects her comparison outright and replaces it with another that seems equally unsatisfactory ("I don't know what else to call it"). Teresa repeatedly affirms that the mystical experience resists definition, even through analogy. But if we consider these protestations within the context of her general rhetorical strategy, we can see that the "coarse comparisons," the ones that occur to Teresa's "dull wit," are not only a statement about ineffability but also a means of disavowing the presumption of exegesis. By allowing the reader to experience her frustration, indeed, her failure to find *le mot juste*, Teresa succeeds in explaining without teaching.

Scriptural Imprecision

Teresa's earliest biographer, Father Yepes, reported that Teresa once rejected a prospective novice who owned her own Bible, saying, "Bible, daughter? Don't come around here, we don't need you or your Bible, for we are ignorant women and we only know how to spin and do what we are ordered."[10] Although the anecdote may be apocryphal, it does suggest that Teresa was ever mindful of the Index's proscription against vernacular biblical translations. It is not surprising, therefore, that in the precarious atmosphere of 1577 all Teresa's references to Scripture are deliberately imprecise. For example, when she writes of Jacob's ladder, she implies that her source is aural rather than written: "No sé si atino en lo que digo, porque aunque lo he oído no sé si se me acuerda bien" (6:4:395) 'I don't know if I'm guessing right in what I say, for although I have heard this story about Jacob, I don't know if I'm remembering it correctly' (K, p. 128). The notes of imprecision and approximation are pervasive, and, as Hans Flasche has remarked, the verb "parecer" 'to seem' and other expressions of uncertaintly are extremely frequent in this text. When Teresa wishes to explicate the verse "Dilatasti cor meum" from Psalm 118, she writes "Y no me parece que es cosa—como digo—que su nacimiento es del corazón, sino de otra parte aún más interior, como una cosa profunda. Pienso que deve ser el centro del alma, como después he entendido y diré a la postre; que cierto veo secretos en nosotros mesmos que me train espantada muchas veces" (4:2:367) 'I don't think the experience is something, as I say, that rises from the heart, but from another part still more interior, as from something deep. I think this must be the center of the soul, as I later came to understand and will mention at the end. For certainly I see secrets within ourselves that have often caused me to mar-

---

[10] Cited in Edgar Allison Peers, *Studies of the Spanish Mystics*, 2d ed. (London: Macmillan, 1951–), 1: 180, n. 2.

vel' (K, p. 74–75). The repetition of "cosa" 'something,' the formula "me parece" 'it seems to me' and "deve ser" 'must be' stresses the hypothetical nature of her assertion, which nevertheless is resolved into a certainty ("he entendido" 'I came to understand' "cierto veo" 'certainly I see') based on personal experience.[11]

At one point Teresa explicitly calls attention to this strategy: "Siempre en cosas dificultosas, aunque me parece que lo entiendo y que digo verdad, voy con este lenguaje de que 'me parece'; porque si me engañare, estoy muy aparejada a creer lo que dijeren los que tienen letras muchas" (5:1:374) 'In difficult matters even though it seems to me that I understand and that I speak the truth, I always use this expression "it seems to me." For if I am mistaken, I'm very much prepared to believe what those who have a great deal of learning say' (K, p. 88). Another recurrent formula noted by Flasche is the untranslatable play on words produced by pairing *atinar/desatinar*.[12] Teresa continually protests that she will not be able to "get it right" (*atinar*), that she will end up saying "nonsense" (*desatinar*): "¡Oh secretos de Dios, que no me hartaría de procurar dar a entenderlos si pensase acertar en algo!, y ansí diré mil desatinos, por si alguna vez atinase, para que alabemos mucho a el Señor" (5:1:374) 'Oh secrets of God! I would never tire of trying to explain them if I thought I could in some way manage to do so; thus I will say a thousand foolish things in order that I might at times succeed and that we might give great praise to the Lord' (K, p. 87).

[11] Hans Flasche, "El problema de la certeza en el *Castillo interior*," in *Congreso internacional Teresiano 4–7 octubre, 1982*, ed. Teófanes Egido Martínez et al. (Salamanca: Universidad de Salamanca, 1983), 2: 447–458; quotation p. 451. At another point Teresa simultaneously confesses her ignorance and claims a charismatic ability to understand vernacular Scripture: "No ha sido poco hacer Su Majestad que entienda yo qué quiere decir el romance de este verso a este tiempo, según soy torpe en este caso" (3:1:357) 'His Majesty has done no small thing in giving me understanding right now of what this verse means in the vernacular, for I am ignorant in matters like this' (K, p. 55).

[12] Flasche, "El problema," 2: 447.

Structural Improvisation

Teresa also underscores the improvisational nature of the composition of the text. She apologizes for her digressions and distractions: "No sé a qué propósito he dicho esto, hermanas, ni para qué, que no me he entendido" (6:6:401) 'I don't know what my goal was in saying this, Sisters, nor why I said it, for these words were not planned' (K, p. 139); "Pareceros ha, hermanas, que hablo fuera de propósito . . ." (3:2:360) 'It must seem to you, Sisters, that I'm not staying on the subject . . .' (K, p. 62). Then she reorients her readers (and herself) with expressions such as "Pues tornando a lo que decíamos" (7:2:423) 'Well, to return to what we were saying' (K, p. 181). She notes her inability to revise or even reread and laments her faulty memory: "¡Válame Dios en lo que me he metido! Ya tenía olvidado lo que tratava, porque los negocios y salud me hacen dejarlo a mejor tiempo; y como tengo poca memoria irá todo desconcertado, por no poder tornarlo a leer, y aun quizás se es todo desconcierto cuanto digo. Al menos es lo que siento" (4:2:366) 'God help me with what I have undertaken! I've already forgot what I was dealing with, for business matters and poor health have forced me to set this work aside just when I was at my best; and since I have a poor memory everything will come out confused because I can't go back to read it over. And perhaps even everything else I say is confused; at least that's what I feel it is' (K, p. 73).

In the crush of ideas some things will need to be repeated and others will be related out of sequence: "No llevaré por concierto como suceden, sino como se me ofreciere a la memoria" (6:1:385) 'I will not deal with them according to the order in which they happen, but as they come to mind' (K, p. 109). Some images disappear and reappear from time to time in an almost aleatory manner: 'No penséis que la tengo olvidada' "Don't think I have forgotten it" (K, p. 166), Teresa remarks, as she again returns to the comparison of the soul as butterfly. In sum, Teresa repeatedly denies possessing any literary skill, much less theological certainty or authority. Disorder, digression, and imprecision—these are the tactics that disguise a charismatic text as women's chatter.

FROM MILES CHRISTI TO SPONSA CHRISTI

The desire to disavow the literary status of her text may explain why Teresa never used the world "*alegoría*," preferring "*comparación*" instead. As noted earlier, Teresa ironically denigrates "*comparaciones*" in the first *morada* as a necessary device for explaining difficult concepts to dull women. And we have seen that she repeatedly expresses her dissatisfaction with her comparisons, which are never "quite right." But if comparisons are a woman's provisional technique, they need not be held up to the standards of consistency that allegory demands.

Helmut Hatzfeld and Víctor de la Concha have attempted to explain the inconsistencies of Teresa's allegorical structure in terms of aesthetic preference. According to Hatzfeld, Teresa works through a technique of catachresis, or deliberately paradoxical figures of speech: "She shrewdly is aware from the beginning of her catachrestic image, according to which the soul has to enter into herself, . . . becoming bridal chamber and spouse at the same time."[13] De la Concha has described her technique as one of concatenation or branching association: the image of the castle serves as an axis upon which related images (the soul as butterfly and dove, the soul as a garden watered by God) are inscribed.[14] Recently Catherine Swietlicki has suggested the influence of cabala, which Teresa may have learned directly from her *converso* family or absorbed indirectly from folk sources. She notes in particular coincidences with the thirteenth-century *Sefer ha-Zohar* in Tere-

---

[13] Helmut Hatzfeld, *Santa Teresa de Avila* (New York: Twayne, 1968), p. 43.

[14] de la Concha, *El arte literario de Santa Teresa* (Barcelona: Ariel, 1978), pp. 272, 247.

sa's concepts of the silkworm, the mirror, the palm, and interior mansions. Teresa's seemingly unsystematic structure, Swietlicki adds, may also be attributed to cabalistic influence: "The manner in which she transforms and interweaves these images is like that of Zoharic stylistics, in which mixing metaphors and interrelating simultaneous symbol systems is considered an art."[15]

Teresa's mixed metaphors also reflect her attempt to combine two major allegories of medieval monastic life, the *miles Christi* and the *sponsa Christi*. The first three *moradas* are based on a monastic motif that found renewed significance in Counter-Reformation Spain—the Christian soul conceived as a soldier who must fight actively against evil from within and temptation from without. In the first *morada* the soul as warrior, aided by vassals (the senses and faculties), battles against internal snakes and vermin in an effort to protect the King (Christ) who dwells in the castle's inner sanctum. In the second *morada* the devil wages even more intense warfare, the artillery strikes are louder, the soul must be "manly." In the third *morada*, even though initial battles have been won, the soul must continue to "walk in fear." Like someone whose enemy is at the door, the soul must sleep and eat with arms at its side. But once past the initial sections of the third *morada*, the militaristic imagery largely disappears. In fact, the major trial at this stage—spiritual dryness—has no equivalent in the military allegory and is explained by means of an economic parable and with images of pilgrimage. The pilgrim's road (*camino*) has replaced the soldier's battle. In the fourth *morada* Teresa again takes up military imagery to describe the prayer of recollection, but it merges into a new pastoral image: the senses, "people of the castle" who have grown used to walking around outside of it with

---

[15] Swietlicki, *Spanish Christian Cabala*, p. 51. Swietlicki is not suggesting judaizing on Teresa's part, noting that cabalistic symbolism had long been incorporated by Christian apologists. She proposes rather that Teresa's cabalistic knowledge may have been absorbed unwittingly at a folk level (pp. 44–51, 156).

its enemies, are drawn back into the dwelling place/castle by the whistle of a benevolent shepherd/King (4:2:368).[16] At this stage Teresa begins to interweave water imagery and the comparison of the soul as a silkworm—spinning its cocoon, dying to the world, reborn in Christ. The reason for abandoning militaristic imagery is clear: the spiritual delights beyond the third *morada* cannot be sought; penance, good works, and prayer are necessary but insufficient conditions for spiritual favors. Militaristic imagery is obviously incompatible with the "peacefulness" of this spiritual state: "estas obras interiores son todas suaves y pacíficas, y hacer cosa penosa, antes daña que aprovecha" (4:3:370) 'these interior works are all gentle and peaceful; doing something arduous would cause more harm than good' (K, p. 80). A series of more passive images follows: the soldier/pilgrim becomes the lost lamb, the beggar at the gate, the drunkard, the fool, and the silkworm. In a striking image the soul is compared to a baby at the breast: "[N]o está aún el alma criada, sino como un niño que comienza a mamar, que si se aparta de los pechos de su madre, ¿qué se puede esperar de él sino la muerte?" (4:3:371) 'The soul is not yet grown but is like a suckling child. If it turns away from its mother's breast, what can be expected for it but death?' (K, p. 82).[17] Finally the image of the soul as Bride appears.

Again, scriptural references are defensively vague:

[16] Fernández has remarked that after the first four *moradas* the term *castillo* with its connotations of struggle and battle is replaced by *morada*, which connotes repose ("Génesis y estructura de *Las moradas*," 2: 619, 622).

[17] For a discussion of the motif of the suckling soul and the maternal Christ see John Bugge, *"Virginitas": An Essay in the History of a Medieval Ideal* (The Hague: Martinus-Nijhoff, 1975); Carolyn Bynum, *Jesus as Mother: Studies in the Spirituality of the High Middle Ages* (Berkeley: University of California Press, 1982), and *Holy Feast and Holy Fast: The Religious Significance of Food to Medieval Women* (Berkeley: University of California Press, 1987). Although Teresa's maternal imagery is restrained in comparison with some of the late medieval texts cited by Bynum, in the Spain of 1577 even her oblique references to the suckling soul were audacious.

"Ahora me acuerdo sobre esto que digo de que no somos parte, de lo que havéis oído que dice la esposa en los Cantares: 'Llevóme el rey a la bodega del vino, u metióme,' creo que dice" (5:1:375) 'Now I recall, in saying that we have no part to play, what you have heard the Bride say in the *Song of Songs*: "He brought me into the wine cellar" (or placed me there, I believe it says)' (K, p. 90). Teresa apologetically refers to the new train of imagery she will now develop as another "coarse comparison": "Ya ternéis oído muchas veces que se desposa Dios con las almas espiritualmente. . . . Y aunque sea grosera comparación, yo no hallo otra que más pueda dar a entender lo que pretendo, que el sacramento del matrimonio" (5:4:382) 'You've already often heard that God espouses souls spiritually. . . . And even though the comparison may be a coarse one I cannot find another that would better explain what I mean than the sacrament of marriage' (K, p. 103).

In spite of her professed reluctance, nuptial mysticism begins to emerge as the crucial allegory of the final three books of *The Interior Castle*. As the future Bride, the soul's spiritual progress follows the sequence of marriage arrangements in Teresa's day: (1) the meeting between young man and woman, (2) the exchange of gifts, (3) betrothal, (4) marriage. Certain terms of militaristic allegory find a new semantic value within the context of the epithalamium: courage is needed, not to wage battle, but to overcome shyness with the Bridegroom. The soul is wounded, not by the devil's vipers, but by the Spouse's arrow of love: "[P]arece le llega a las entrañas esta pena y que cuando de ellas saca la saeta el que la hiere, verdaderamente parece que se las lleva tras sí, según el sentimiento de amor siente" (6:2: 389) 'It seems this pain reaches to the soul's very depths [entrails] and that when he who wounds it draws out the arrow, it indeed seems in accord with the deep love the soul feels that God is drawing these very depths after Him' (K, p. 116). Erotic pain replaces that of worldly trials: "[E]s harta pena, aunque sabrosa y dulce" (6:2:389) 'The pain is great, although delightful and sweet' (K, p. 116). In fact, it is the combination of pleasure and pain which assures the soul that the experience is not diabolical.

As the soul's gender is transformed, the spatial orientation of the allegory is also reversed; the soul does not guard against invasion from the outer walls—the Bridegroom orders the walls be closed off so that He can be alone with the Bride; the soul is drawn effortlessly and irresistibly to the center, penetrated by gentle touches: "[M]e parece eran bien empleados cuantos trabajos se pasan por gozar de estos toques de su amor tan suaves y penetrativos" (7:3:426) '[I]t seems to me that all the trials endured for the sake of enjoying these touches of His love, so gentle and penetrating would be well worthwhile' (K, p. 185).

Several passages in the seventh *morada* are particularly allusive to the *Canticles*. "Estos efectos . . . da Dios cuando llega el alma a Sí, con este ósculo que pedía la Esposa" (7:3:427) 'These effects . . . are given by God when he brings the soul to Himself with this kiss sought by the bride' (K, p. 187); "[E]sforzado [el cuerpo] con esfuerzo que tiene el alma beviendo el vino de esta bodega adonde la ha traído su Esposo" (7:4:429) 'But the soul is fortified by the strength it has from drinking wine in this wine cellar, where its Spouse has brought it' (K, pp. 191–192). Momentarily Teresa fuses the maternal imagery, introduced in the fourth *morada*, with the erotic language of the *Canticles*: "[D]e aquellos pechos divinos, adonde parece está Dios siempre sustentando el alma, salen unos rayos de leche que toda la gente del castillo conorta" (7:2:423) 'For from those divine breasts where it seems God is always sustaining the soul there flow streams of milk bringing comfort to all the people of the castle' (K, pp. 179–180). But in general Teresa seems to be able to avoid close scriptural paraphrase of the *Canticles* through her concatenation of fragmentary biblical allusions. The passage referring to the kiss of the Bridegroom continues: "Aquí se dan las aguas a esta cierva que va herida, en abundancia. Aquí se deleita en el tabernáculo de Dios. Aquí halla la paloma que envió Noé a ver si era acabada la tempestad, la oliva. . . . ¡Oh, Jesús, y quién supiera las muchas cosas de la Escritura que deve haver para dar a entender esta paz del alma!" (7:3:427) 'Here an abundance of water is given to this deer that was wounded. Here one delights in God's tabernacle. Here the dove Noah sent out to see if the storm was over finds the olive branch. . . . Oh Jesus! Who would know the many things there must be in Scripture to explain this peace of soul!' (K, p. 187). Teresa judiciously has retreated from the most telling symbol of the *Canticles* into the protective cover of professed ignorance and scriptural imprecision.

The Language of Erotic Spirituality

Noting Teresa's intermittent use of the language of erotic spirituality, Helmut Hatzfeld concluded that the mystical marriage "did not possess for St. Teresa a necessary mystical reality" but was rather a metaphorical description equivalent to many others of her own invention.[18] This position is untenable in the light of Teresa's reported vision of November 18, 1572. She writes that Christ appeared before her, saying as he gave her his right hand, "Mira este clavo, que es señal que serás mi esposa desde hoy" (*Cuentas de conciencia*, no. 25a, p. 446) 'Behold this nail, which is a sign that from this day you will be My spouse' (my translation). The *sponsa Christi* was not just a literary motif but rather a psychic reality for Teresa. The "disorder" of *The Interior Castle*, with its catachrestic imagery and semantic reversals, undoubtedly can be attributed to Teresa's desire to synthesize elements from many different sources— Western and perhaps Semitic. But her reasons for imbedding the language of the *Canticles* in a profusion of com-

[18] Hatzfeld, *Estudios literarios sobre mística española* (Madrid: Gredos, 1955), p. 176.

peting imagery are also pragmatic. In 1577 obfuscation was safer than clarity.

An obvious danger was that the more Teresa echoed the language of the *Song of Songs*, the more she exposed herself to the charge of interpreting Scripture, and, as we have seen, the Index of 1559 was nothing if not explicit in this regard. Expressly prohibited were "any and all sermons, letters, treatises, prayers, or other writings which speak of or treat the Holy Scriptures."[19] Nonetheless, between 1566 and 1567, Teresa herself had written a brief work inspired by several verses of the *Song of Songs*. In this text, variously known as *Meditations on the Song of Songs* and *Conceptions of Love of God*, Teresa was careful not to claim the right to interpret Scripture; but she did slyly suggest that women, by virtue of their limited intellect, have the capacity to enjoy a fragmentary, passive, and ineffable experience of Scripture. She argued that women understand the Scriptures differently from men—that they must surrender themselves to an effortless understanding without "wearing themselves out" trying to understand as men must.[20] Furthermore, the verses upon which Teresa bases her meditations are the most erotic of the *Canticles*: "Let Him kiss me with a Kiss of His mouth" and "Thy breasts are better than wine for they give off fragrance of sweet odours." Nor do Teresa's commentaries shy away from the eroticism inherent in the langauge of these verses:

> Mas cuando este Esposo riquísimo la quiere enriquecer y regalar más, conviértela tanto en Sí, que, como una persona que el gran placer y contento la desmaya, le parece se queda suspendida en aquellos divinos brazos y arrimada a aquel

[19] *Indice de Valdés* (1559), cited by Antonio Márquez, *Literatura e Inquisición en España* (Madrid: Taurus, 1980), p. 104.

[20] See Carole Slade's arguments that Teresa here develops a distinctly feminine hermeneutics in "Saint Teresa's *Meditaciones sobre los cantares*: The Hermeneutics of Humility and Enjoyment," *Religion and Literature* 18 (1986): 27–43.

sagrado costado y aquellos pechos divinos. No sabe más de gozar, sustentada con aquella leche divina, que la va criando su Esposo y mejorando para poderla regalar y que merezca cada día más. Cuando despierta de aquel sueño y de aquella embriaguez celestial, queda como cosa espantada y embobada y con un santo desatino.   (*Meditaciones*, ch. 4, p. 335)

But when this most wealthy Spouse desires to enrich and comfort the Bride still more, He draws her so closely to Him that she is like one who swoons from excess of pleasure and joy and seems to be suspended in those Divine arms and drawn near to that sacred side and to those Divine breasts. Sustained by that Divine milk with which her Spouse continually nourishes her and growing in grace so that she may be enabled to receive His comforts, she can do nothing but rejoice. Awakening from that sleep and heavenly inebriations, she is like one amazed and stupefied.[21]

Again we see the conflation of Christ as spouse and mother, in a way that reveals the inadequacy of "erotic" as a description of the blissful symbiosis with a divine matrix. In this text Teresa not only defends women's right to be inspired by the language of the *Canticles*, she ridicules those who prudishly reject it: "Pareceros ha que hay algunas en estos Cánticos que se pudieran decir por otro estilo. Según es nuestra torpeza, no me espantaría. He oído a algunas personas decir que antes huían de oírlas. ¡Oh, válame Dios, que gran miseria es la nuestra!" (*Meditaciones*, ch. 1, p. 323) 'You may think that in these *Canticles* there are some things which might have been said in a different way. We are so stupid that I should not be surprised if you did: I have heard some people say that they actually tried not to listen to them. O God, what miserable creatures we are!' (Peers, CW, 2: 360). In the *Meditations* Teresa unequivocally champions the language of maternal/erotic

[21] *Meditations on the Song of Songs*, in *The Complete Works of Saint Teresa of Jesus*, trans. E. Allison Peers, 3 vols. (London: Sheed and Ward, 1944–1946), 2: 384; hereafter abbreviated as Peers, CW.

spirituality as the "language spoken by the Holy Spirit," as God's "deliberately chosen style."[22] This audacious text was copied and circulated among the Disalced nuns but did not receive Báñez' official approbation until 1575. Apparently when Teresa began the *Meditations* in the late 1560s, she felt secure enough under the protection of Carmelite General Rubeo to allow the diffusion of an "underground text." But by the time she began *The Interior Castle* in 1577, as we have seen, the situation had changed dramatically. In the earlier work it is clear that Teresa found in the most highly charged verses of the *Canticles* a stimulus for mystical contemplation; but in the later text she could only make veiled references to the language of erotic spirituality. Her caution was not unwarranted: in 1580 she received the order to burn the *Meditations*. As Gracián summarizes the anonymous censor's objections:

> She was ordered to burn this book, since it seemed to a certain confessor of hers very unorthodox and dangerous for a woman to write about the *Song of Songs*. He was moved by his pious concern that, as St. Paul says, women should be silent in God's church, which is to say: they should not preach from the pulpit, or teach at universities, or print books. And since at the time Luther's heresy was doing much harm, for it had opened the doors for ignorant women and men to read and explicate divine works, . . . it seemed to him that the book should be burned. And so, as soon as this priest ordered it, she threw her book into the fire, practicing her two heroic virtues of humility and obedience.[23]

[22] Teresa variously characterizes the language of the *Canticles* as "invenciones" (inventions), "lenguaje dicho por el Espíritu Santo" (the language spoken by the Holy Spirit), and "estilo" (style) (*Meditaciones*, Ch. 1, p. 323). In the same chapter she also relates her shock at hearing an audience react with laughter to a sermon on the Bride's converse with God.

[23] *Obras completas*, nueva revisión del texto original con notas críticas, ed. Efrén de la Madre de Dios, Otilio de Niño Jesús, and Otger Steggink, 3 vols. (Madrid: Católica, 1951–1959), 2: 579, my translation. Four copies,

Exegesis of the *Canticles* had always been problematical, and this was no more true than during the 1570s in Spain. During the Middle Ages two alternative interpretations had enjoyed an uneasy coexistence. The Originist, or pneumatic allegory of the individual soul's marriage to Christ, flourished in the monastic tradition, whereas the Augustinian, or ecclesiological exegesis of the Church as Christ's bride, was favored by the Scholastic tradition.[24] However, theologians in Counter-Reformation Spain were inclined to view anything other than ecclesiological exegesis as nonallegorical or "literal." The great biblical scholar Friar Luis de León was imprisoned from 1572 to 1575 by the Inquisition for questioning the accuracy of the Vulgate and for translating the *Song of Songs* into Spanish. He was castigated not only for the act of translation itself but also for the "literalness" of his translation and commentary: he had paid scant attention to the ecclesiological allegory, mentioning it almost in passing. One witness testified that the work seemed to him "nothing but a love letter, in no way spiritual, differing hardly at all from the love poems of Ovid."[25] Fray Luis had indeed rendered the original Hebrew in plain, contemporary Spanish (using words such as *besos* or kisses and *pechos* or breasts), and the unveiled eroticism made his critics decidedly uncom-

in various stages of completeness, did survive the order. Gracián's comments first appeared in the 1611 edition. It is hardly surprising that Friar Luis omitted the *Meditations* from his princeps edition of 1582.

[24] Bugge, *Virginitas*, pp. 56–59, 90–96. Also consult Pierre Adnés, "Mariage spirituel," in *Diccionnaire de spiritualité, ascétique et mystique*, ed. M. Viller et al. (Paris: Beauchesne, 1977), 10: 389–408. For the rise of *Braudmystik* or nuptial mysticism in the late Middle Ages see Bynum, *Holy Feast*, pp. 26, 28, 150–152. Swietlicki notes the special fondness of Judaic cabalists for the *Song of Songs* and suggests cabalistic influence on the nuptial mysticism of Teresa and Juan de la Cruz (*Spanish Christian Cabala*, pp. 169–171).

[25] *Proceso original que la Inquisición de Valladolid hizo al marstro Fr. Luis de León*, ed. Miguel Salvá and Pedro Sainz de Baranda, vol. 10 of Colección de Documentos inéditos para la historia de España (Madrid: Viuda de Calero, 1847), p. 27.

fortable. That the translation was prepared for a woman, the nun Isabel Osorio, only aggravated his problems: "The [*Canticles*] should not be allowed to circulate in the romance tongue, especially among women, for whom this exposition appears to have been written."[26] Luis, however, was not a "literalist" in the sense that he thought the *Canticles* were "nothing but" a secular epithalamium. This *converso* scholar simply gave precedence to the pneumatic over the ecclesiological component of the allegory. He therefore felt that it was necessary to render fully the eroticism of the original Hebrew, because he argued, like Teresa, that this was the language chosen by the Holy Spirit to communicate God's love for man.[27]

Objections very similar to those brought against Friar Luis were raised when Teresa's works were examined posthumously. One theologian was disturbed by the explicitness of her language, which he described, paradoxically, as being both "hyperbolic" and "literal": "And this is something I cannot excuse, that by using hyperbole she puts down the literal meaning of the Holy Scripture, instead of other true meanings it has in itself, without hyperboles."[28] It is interesting, in this light, that Teresa twice revised her wording in *The Interior Castle* because it may have seemed too explicit: in *morada* seven she originally

---

[26] Ibid., p. 26.

[27] Swietlicki attributes Luis's sensuality to the cabalistic tradition of the *Zohar*, with its emphasis on divine sexuality and the sanctity of the physical union in marriage (*Spanish Christian Cabala*, p. 118). Also see Víctor García de la Concha, "Exposición del *Cantar de los cantares*," in *Academia literaria renascentista*, vol. 1, *Fray Luis de León*, ed. Víctor García de la Concha (Salamanca: Ediciones Universidad de Salamanca, 1981), pp. 171–192. De la Concha notes that in 1580, under considerable pressure, Luis rewrote his commentaries and expanded the ecclesiological allegory. The three Canticle-inspired poems of St. John of the Cross were probably written while he was in jail in 1577 but were not published until 1618, twenty-seven years after his death. As Marcel Bataillon notes, John, like Teresa, was suspected of Illuminism in his lifetime (*Erasmo y España*, trans. Antonio Alatorre, 2d rev. ed. [1966; reprint ed., Mexico: Fondo de cultura económica, 1982], p. 759).

[28] Llamas, *Santa Teresa*, p. 468.

referred to "those who have consummated marriage" and then changed her text to read "two who can no longer be separated" (K, p. 178). For Counter-Reformation theologians the "true meaning" of the *Canticles* was the ecclesiological allegory; they did not wish to be reminded of the erotic language of the original text.

The distrust of erotic spirituality in Counter-Reformation Spain is a topic that deserves a study of its own. It may be related to a general phenomenon in Reformation and Counter-Reformation Europe alike—the increasing tendency to associate sexuality with the demonic.[29] In the 1570s Spain witnessed a another "outbreak" of Illuminism in Andalucia and Extremadura. Although the Inquisitors saw the new heresy as a continuation of the condemned evangelical piety of the 1520s and 1530s, this time they placed decidedly more emphasis on its supposed orgiastic component. According to the Inquisition's documents, Illuminist doctrine held that "kissing and indecent touchings are not a sin."[30] The beatas of Llerena, who were ultimately condemned in an *auto da fe* in 1579, reported erotic visons of Christ's humanity and an "intimate union with God."[31] With the prosecution of the Llerena group the practice of mental prayer and the desire for union with God were more closely linked with the heresy of sexual

[29] In particular, witchcraft was redefined in terms of women's sexual allegiance to Satan. Recently a number of historians of the sixteenth century have described the witch hunts as symptomatic of a dramatic increase in misogyny during this period. See Joseph Klaits, *Servants of Satan: The Age of the Witch Hunts* (Bloomington: Indiana University Press, 1986), pp. 52–77; H. C. Erik Midelfort, *Witch Hunting in Southwestern Germany, 1562–1682* (Stanford, Ca.: Stanford University Press, 1972), pp. 195–196; and Rosemary Ruether, "The Persecution of Witches: A Case of Sexism and Agism," *Christianity and Crisis* 34 (1974): 291–295.

[30] Bernardino Llorca, *La Inquisición española y los alumbrados (1509–1667)* (Salamanca: Universidad Pontíficia, 1980), p. 114, n. 24. Also see Alvaro Huerga's three-volume *Historia de los alumbrados (1570–1630)* (Madrid: Fundación universitaria española, 1978).

[31] Llorca, *Inquisición*, pp. 103–121. With priestly delicacy Llorca declines to transcribe the descriptions of the beatas' visions of Christ's humanity because they are "too realistic" (p. 298).

impeccability. Although there is reason to doubt that such excesses actually took place, the important point is that especially after 1575 a growing sector interpreted ecstatic trances as a cover for literal sexual activity. The fact that many beatas confidently referred to themselves as "Christ's brides" cast doubt on any expression of nuptial mysticism.[32]

We can see from Alonso de la Fuente's affidavit against *The Interior Castle* that Teresa did not escape association with these groups: "And we saw the same thing with our own eyes in more than twenty towns of Extremadura, where a multitude of men and women had ecstacies and fainted and felt the presence of God and all the effects that are described here in Teresa's works. And if the woman was a prostitute and ignorant, she was all the more subject to such effects and felt them more readily."[33] In Teresa's particular case rumors of sexual improprieties in the Seville convent (to be discussed in the next chapter) only aggravated matters.

Teresa had undoubtedly taken risks in the late 1560s when she began the *Meditations*, and the risks were considerably greater after the Discalced lost papal support. It seems clear, nonetheless, that Teresa, who found herself on the frontiers of contemporary orthodoxy, nevertheless felt the idea of spiritual marriage so crucial that she was willing to continue to take these risks. Although her erotic language is more concealed in the later text, she was unwilling to abandon it altogether. In Teresa's mind surrender to and union with a masculine/maternal other was more than a comparison; it was the substance of the experience of the seventh *morada*.

---

[32] A 1588 trial records that Gaspar Lucas, an Illuminist "master and dogmatizer," owned a heavily marked copy of a "suspect" book by the great Flemmish mystic Ruysbroeck—in all likelihood his *De ornatu spiritualium nuptiarum* (Alvaro Huerga, "Las lecturas místicas de los alumbrados," in *Santa Teresa y la literatura mística hispánica*, ed. Manuel Criado de Val [Madrid: EDI–6, 1984], pp. 571–581; quotation p. 579).

[33] Llamas, *Santa Teresa*, p. 406.

The inconsistencies in the allegory—the soul's transformation from male to female, soldier to bride, the movement from struggle to surrender, from active to passive penetration—reflect the theologically precarious position of Teresa's mysticism, that is, her need to disavow the heresy of *dejamiento* and assert her conviction that mystical experiences are ultimately gratuitous. The allegory of the soul as soldier defending a castle, as appropriate as it was for the Counter-Reformation insistence on works, was ultimately an inadequate vehicle for the description of the intimate union. Teresa was surely aware that the imagery of the spiritual marriage was not "coarse" but dangerous, and she clothed it in "feminine" confusion and a proliferation of conflicting comparisons. Her rhetoric of obfuscation both conceals and protects the Bride of *The Interior Castle*.

Chapter V

THE BOOK OF FOUNDATIONS AND THE RHETORIC OF AUTHORITY

ONE OF the central paradoxes of Teresa's life is that she fought so long and so persistently against hierarchical authority precisely in order to return her order to a much more authoritarian monastic rule. It is not surprising, therefore, that *The Book of Foundations*, Teresa's account of the founding of sixteen Discalced convents, is marked by a profound ambivalence to authority. Teresa the reformer and Teresa the Mother Foundress have very different stories to tell that rest on different premises about the relationship between the individual and authority. In one strand of her narrative Teresa is the picaresque protagonist of a series of road adventures, a wily outsider who prevails through wit and determination. In another strand she is the omniscient narrator of exemplary tales about rebel daughters, for whom surrender to authority is eventually rewarded. The two narratives are never completely reconciled; rather each tends to challenge the authority of the opposing voice, betraying its defensive fictions and significant silences.

LEAVING HOME

We have seen that Teresa's adolescence was marked by two departures from her father's home. On the first occasion she was "expelled" for suspicion of sexual misconduct; on the second occasion she ran away from home under cover of night to join a convent against her father's wishes. Although disparate on the surface level, both departures can be seen as motivated by Teresa's need to break with her father. As revealed in *The Book of Her Life*, Teresa felt intense guilt over her natural attractiveness, an attractiveness that had inspired a possessive love in her father. Much of her psychological history can be seen as a repeated "leaving home"—as a response to her continued need to rebel or to break affective ties with successive authority figures. However, the guilt produced by each act of rebellion tended to trigger a rapprochement with authority, resulting, in turn, in renewed guilt over intimacy. Teresa's enormous efforts as a reformer of her order can be seen in themselves as instances of this history of repetition, as a rebellious "leaving home" to search for an ideal home.

It is essential to note that as a reformer Teresa encountered extreme opposition. Her reform effort represented a break with the traditional system that bound religious orders to powerful elites through a system of endowed chaplaincies. She stubbornly insistented on founding her convents in poverty, that is, without an endowment, in order to ensure her nuns' detachment from the demands of secular elites and in particular their freedom to practice contemplative prayer as opposed to vocal prayers chanted for the souls of benefactors.[1] The economic consequence of this decision was resistence from the municipalities that were to be the sites of the new convents. The smaller the town, and the greater the number of other convents and monasteries in the vicinity, the greater was the antagonism to an additional economic burden. Teresa's benefactors, who either bought or arranged to rent houses for her, also frequently faced hostility from relatives who resented a diversion of family capital. An insistence on poverty also implied criticism of ecclesiastic cupidity and thus "Protestant" inclinations. As Márquez Villanueva has pointed out, in the anti-Semitic environment of sixteenth-century Castile the fact that many of Teresa's patrons were

---

[1] Jodi Bilinkoff, "The Social Meaning of Religious Reform: The Case of St. Teresa and Avila," *Archiv für Reformationsgeschichte* 79 (1988): 340–357.

wealthy *converso* merchants contributed to the hostility toward the Carmelite reform.[2] Another obvious obstacle was the general suspicion of contemplative prayer. Even Teresa's personal supporters were skeptical of her plans to found convents where more women would be encouraged to engage in the debated practice. Finally, internal power struggles within the Carmelite order and rivalry with other orders undoubtedly intensified opposition. As we have seen, the general of the Carmelites turned against the Discalced in 1576, and for the next four years Teresa's reform efforts came to a halt as she was effectively a prisoner at the Toledo convent.

The rigors of reforming an order would appear to have been insurmountable for a frail women in her fifties. In addition to the deplorable traveling conditions of the period Teresa faced mundane problems of finding suitable houses, modifying them to accommodate a chapel, and securing donations for basic furnishings. At every step she was forced to confront reluctant, often hostile authorities, both civil and religious. But from Teresa's point of view the foundations were part of a religious quest. Her authority was divine; difficulties were either God-given trials or manifestations of the devil's jealousy. But as *The Book of Foundations* as well as her voluminous correspondence during this period reveal, for Teresa the experience of confronting authority was as exhilarating as her conviction that the foundations were part of a divine quest.

THE SELF-DEPRECIATING HISTORIAN

When Teresa takes up her pen to write the story of these foundations, she writes with a security that was impossi-

[2] For example, Teresa alludes to the particular difficulties surrounding the Toledo foundation because her patrons, the family of the wealthy merchant Martín Ramírez, "no eran ilustres y cavalleros" 'were not illustrious and gentlemen.' See Francisco Márquez Villanueva, "Santa Teresa y el linaje," in *Espiritualidad y literatura en el siglo XVI* (Madrid: Alfaguara, 1968), esp. pp. 141–145 and 152–160.

ble for her to assume when she was writing about contemplative prayer or her mystical experiences. As chronicler of the reform, she is on surer ground than she was as a female religious teacher. Her authority as a historian is, nevertheless, relative. A dual audience is assumed here as in her previous works: she faces an immediate audience of sympathetic contemplative nuns and priests and a potential audience of political enemies. There were many topics that could not be addressed and others that needed to be treated with reticence and tact. Many of the principal characters in the conflict were still alive, and Teresa could not afford to antagonize patrons or political allies. The struggles between the Calced and Discalced were increasingly vindictive. Teresa was understandably evasive about the major battles of the reform and reserved her candor for the relatively minor skirmishes. She was also undoubtedly aware that, in spite of her success, her physical freedom during the years of the foundations represented a contravention of the rulings of the Council of Trent, which insisted that nuns remain confined to their convents. We have already seen that, in the eyes of the Papal Nuncio Felipe Sega, she was a "restless, wandering female."

Although Teresa need not defend herself against charges of usurping the male didactic role in this text, she nonetheless betrays a certain defensiveness about her administrative authority and her assumption of ecclesiastical leadership. She may have considered herself a female Moses, but this was a role she could only allude to. It is not surprising, therefore, that in the Prologue of 1573, she repeats familiar humility topics, although the posture of hyperbolic self-abasement is absent: she professes to write at the command of her confessor Father Ripalda; poor health and her many responsibilities make writing an onerous task; she complains of her "heavy" style, fears she will bore her readers, and trusts that their affection will make them tolerant. She alludes to her poor memory, poor wit, and "*grosería*" or coarseness, but there are no references in the Prologue to her "great sins" or "wretchedness" and her life as a "bad example" that we find, for example, in *The Book of Her Life* and *The Way of Perfection*. But it is understandable that she should disavow her role as the architect of the reform with the self-depreciating diminutive: "Estos medios yo no los procurava, antes me parecía desatino; porque una mujercilla tan sin poder como yo, bien entendía que no podía hacer nada; mas cuando al alma vienen estos deseos, no es en su mano desecharlos. El amor de contentar a Dios y la fe hacen posible lo que por razón natural no lo es"[3] 'I did not seek these things for myself; it seemed to me foolish to do so, for I saw clearly that a [silly] woman such as I, entirely without influence, could do nothing. But when these desires come to the soul it is impossible to drive them away. Faith and the love of pleasing God make possible what according to natural reason is not so.'[4] Thus, in Teresa's account of all her activity, of all her agonized decisions and her battles with bishops and landlords, we find periodic protestations of helplessness and incompetence: "¡Oh, grandeza de Dios, y cómo mostráis vuestro poder en dar osadía a una hormiga!" (ch. 2, p. 502) 'Oh, greatness of God! How dost Thou show forth Thy power in giving such boldness to a mere ant!' (Peers, *CW*, 3: 7). But Teresa also resorts to her old tactic of embracing her opponents' criticisms with comic effect: "Pues ya que tenía licencia, no tenía casa ni blanca para comprarla. Pues crédito para fiarme en nada, si el Señor no le diera, ¿cómo le havía de tener una romera como yo?" (ch. 3, p. 502) 'I now had the licence, but I had neither a house

---

[3] *Libro de las fundaciones*, in *Obras Completas*, edición manual, ed. Efrén de la Madre de Dios and Otger Steggink, (Madrid: Católica, 1962), ch. 2, p. 501. All Spanish citations from Teresa's works in this chapter follow this edition, hereafter abbreviated as *Obras 1962*.

[4] *The Complete Works of Saint Teresa of Jesus*, trans. E. Allison Peers, 3 vols. (London: Shead and Ward, 1944–1946), 3: 6. Although Peers' translation of *Foundations* is excellent, because of his deference to the Saint's dignity his translation is sometimes excessively formal. For some passages I have made variations indicated by brackets and at times substituted my own versions, which may sound anachronistically modern, but I believe they better convey the humorous tone of Teresa's language.

nor so much as a farthing for buying one. And as for credit to go upon, how could a gadabout like myself have any unless the Lord gave it?' (Peers, CW, 3: 8). Peers, who appreciated the humor of the remark, explains that he translated *romera*, literally female pilgrim, as "gadabout," since many pilgrimages in Spain were "quite frankly only outings, or excursions" (Peers, CW, 3: 8, n. 5).

PICARESQUE HISTORY

Thus, although Teresa is less defensive here about her role as writer, political considerations make it necessary for her to avoid highlighting her role as a leader. She engages her readers and wards off censure not only with ironic self-depreciation but also with good-natured self-exposure, repeatedly stressing the incongruity between her meager ability and her surprising success.

In this strand of her history her stance is remarkably antiauthoritarian; indeed, it is picaresque in its mischievous revelations. She slyly reveals that in her determination to do God's work she must rely on her charm, ingenuity, and, at times, deception in order to outwit unenlightened souls, be they landlords, town councilmen, or archbishops. For example, in the battle to gain a foothold in a hostile municipality a favorite tactic was to have a lay friend rent a house on behalf of the nuns, without informing the landlord of the intended purpose of the property. Teresa would then secretly move her nuns into the house under cover of darkness, work through the night cleaning the house, and, if possible, arrange for a consecrated Host to be brought onto the premises. (When the former tenants were untidy students from the University of Salamanca, the house cleaning alone was a formidable task.) By the time the citizens of the town realized what was happening, the existence of another charitable institution was a *fait accompli*. Teresa is willing to include herself as a comic target in describing the ludicrous vicissitudes of these nocturnal escapades. For example, at Medina del Campo Teresa was eager to avoid detection by a group of Augustinian friars, who opposed the founding of a competing religious house so close to their own. She writes, "Llegamos a . . . las doce de la noche; apeámonos en el monesterio de Santa Ana por no hacer ruido, y a pie nos fuimos a la casa. Fue harta misericordia del Señor, que a aquella hora encerravan toros para correr otro día, no nos topar alguno. Con el embevecimiento que llevávamos, no havía acuerdo de nada" (ch. 3, p. 503) 'We arrived . . . at midnight. In order not to make any noise we got off at the monastery of Saint Anne and went to the house on foot. At that time they were bringing in the bulls they were going to run the next day, and, thank God, we didn't run into one. We were so wrapped up in what we were doing that we weren't thinking of anything else' (my translation). Setbacks, misjudgments, and disagreements are related with a humorous drop to a broadly colloquial register: "Con todo, no podía acabar que me diesen esta licencia; porque cuando tenía un poco blando el governador, no lo estavan los del Consejo" (ch. 15, p. 536) 'All in all, I couldn't get them to give me the license, because as soon as I softened up the Governor, the Council went the other way'; "De casa no havía memoria" (ch. 15, p. 536) 'As far as the house is concerned, it was long gone' (my translation).

Some of the anecdotes have an almost farcical quality. In Salamanca, where the nuns have essentially evicted a group of students from the house they were renting, Teresa spends a sleepless All Hallow's Eve with an elderly nun who is as terrified of vengeful students as she is of wandering spirits. In Toledo Teresa and her nuns move into a house secretly at night without informing their fellow tenants. When the nuns arise early for mass the following morning, the terrified tenants naturally assume they are about to be robbed: "Como ellas oyeron golpes, que estavan en la cama, levantáronse despavoridas. Harto tuvimos que hacer en aplacallas; mas ya era hora, que luego se dijo la misa, y aunque estuvieran recias no nos hiceran daño; y como vieron para lo que era, el Señor las aplacó" (ch. 15, pp. 537–538) 'And when they [the tenants] heard the noise—they were in bed—they got up terrified. We had plenty to do to get them to calm down; but it was time for mass, which was said right away, and even though they were hopping mad, they wouldn't do us any harm, and when they saw what it was for, the Lord calmed them down' (my translation). The atmosphere described is one of comic confusion—bumps in the night, mistaken identity, exaggerated fears—all resolved happily in the light of day.

In spite of all her persistence and tact Teresa, in one incident, comes out the worse in a battle of wills with one of her wealthy patronesses. The Princess of Eboli and her husband Ruy Gómez de Silva, had been generous supporters of a monastery and a convent at Pastrana. When Ruy Gómez died in 1573, the princess precipitously decided to enter the Discalced Convent. Teresa was naturally dismayed, knowing the princess's frivolous temperament, but considering her financial contributions there was little that could be done but let her take the veil. The princess moved in with a full retinue of servants and innumerable trinkets, and began to order everyone about. When the prioress protested, the princess (in Teresa's delicately understated expression) "became displeased" with the nuns. In fact, she created so many problems that the nuns preferred beating a hasty retreat from Pastrana to living under the same roof with the capricious aristocrat. The episode is recounted with tactful restraint:

[L]as pobres monjas andavan con tanta inquietud, que yo procuré con cuantas vías pude . . . que quitasen de allí el monesterio, fundándose uno en Segovia . . . adonde se pasaron, dejando cuanto les havía dado la princesa. . . . Las camas y cosillas que las mesmas monjas havían traído, llevaron consigo. . . . Yo con el mayor contento del mundo de verlas en quietud.   (ch. 17, p. 544)

The poor nuns were so upset that I tried . . . in every possible way, to get the convent moved and to have them taken

to Segovia, where a convent was being founded. . . . They
went there, leaving behind everything that the Princess had
given them. . . . The beds and small articles which the nuns
themselves had brought with them they took away. . . . I
myself, when I saw that they were at peace, was the happi-
est person in the world.   (Peers, *CW*, 3: 85)

Teresa neglects to mention the manner in which the spite-
ful princess took her revenge. Earlier Teresa had allowed
a few copies of *The Book of Her Life* to be made for close
friends (much to her confessor Báñez' dismay). Unfortu-
nately, the princess had demanded a copy for herself,
which she circulated indiscriminantly among her mocking
servants. Shortly after the convent was dismantled, she
denounced Teresa's autobiography to the Inquisition.[5]
Given that the princess's outrageous behavior had become
a topic of gossip on a national scale,[6] it seems likely that
Teresa's immediate audience would have been able to appreciate the full impact of her ironic understatement.

Teresa is at her most ironic in Chapter 31, when she describes the founding of the Burgos Convent in 1582. Although the archbishop had initially given his support, he
soon grew lukewarm about the project and eventually opposed it altogether. Teresa nevertheless pressed forward
with the foundation, professing her ignorance of the need
for a current written license. The archbishop was primarily
opposed to a foundation without an endowment—an impediment Teresa circumvented by implicating her patroness in ever increasing financial commitments.[7] The ensu-

---

[5] Although various Inquisitors had reached a favorable decision by
1577, the manuscript remained in Inquisitorial archives until 1588. For the
history of the autograph see the introduction to *Libro de la vida* in *Obras*
1962.

[6] For a full account of the episode, drawing on contemporary correspondence, see Efrén de la Madre de Dios and Otger Steggink, *Tiempo y
vida de Santa Teresa*, 2d rev. ed. (Madrid: Católica, 1977), pp. 585–589.

[7] The patroness, Catalina de Tolosa, was not really free to sign over all
her property to the convent, since she still had living heirs. However,
once the license was granted, Teresa secretly arranged to have a notary
return Catalina's property and deeds. Teresa's *"fait accompli"* tactic nearly

ing tension between Teresa and the archbishop, the archbishop and his old friend the bishop, Teresa and her confessor Gracián, and Teresa and her patroness, turned the business into a comedy of errors. To make things worse, recent floods had made the roads almost impassable, the guides were young and inexperienced, and the normally placid Gracián was terrified of crossing the pontoon bridges ("no se dejó de temer harto" [ch. 31, p. 601] 'he was plenty scared'). Shortly after their arrival the infuriated archbishop suggested that Teresa and her companions leave the city at once. Teresa cannot refrain from remarking sarcastically: "Pues ¡bonitos estaban los caminos, y hacía el tiempo!" (ch. 31 p. 602) 'The roads, of course, were charming, and it was such nice weather!' (Peers, CW, 3: 192). Teresa then comments that this new setback must have been a trial awarded by God for their service but dryly undercuts this piety with "Mas entonces no quisiéramos esta ganancia" (ch. 31, p. 602) 'Just then we were not at all anxious for such a reward' (Peers, CW, 3: 192). Referring to the quarrels between the bishop and archbishop, occasioned by the bishop's support for the foundation, Teresa remarks "[C]omo por la muerte de nuestro Señor se havían hecho amigos los que no lo eran, . . . por mí los había hecho a entrambos enemigos" (ch. 31, p. 607) '[J]ust as people who were not friends had become so through the death of Our Lord, so on my account the Lord had made two who had been friends enemies' (Peers, CW, 3: 202).

Although her tone is obviously facetious, the statement is remarkably self-revelatory. Gracián, in his account of the Burgos founding, is even more frank about Teresa's attitude toward the mechanics of obedience. When he warned her that the archbishop's license was not current, she answered, "Look Father, for God's affairs such prudence and human discretion is not necessary. I know that

---

failed in Segovia, when an enraged vicar-general descended upon the convent chapel and literally dismantled its altar.

in Burgos the Discalced nuns will bring much fruit. Stop your reasoning and let us go there."[8] The Burgos affair marks the culmination of techniques Teresa had perfected in her previous foundations. Her history reveals someone who was extremely adept at dismantling monolithic authority into lesser competing authorities. She had set the precedent during the controversy surrounding the first foundation—pitting her Jesuit confessor against his superior, the Carmelite provincial against the ordinary, the bishop against the municipality, finally circumventing her order's chain of command entirely with an appeal to Rome. Although she always revealed all to her current confessor, she had no qualms about withholding information from other officials when she deemed it advisable— she had also failed to inform the archibishop of Seville that she intended to found an unendowed convent and entirely neglected to tell the vicar-general of Segovia of her plans for foundation. The stated theme for *The Book of Foundations*, "obediens usque ad mortem," is belied by Teresa's dexterity in interpreting ambiguous situations in her favor and in seeking out an authority whose will coincided with her own.

The Book of Foundations is quite simply Teresa's most humorous book—and she is always a very witty writer. When I describe Teresa's history as "picaresque," I am admittedly using the term loosely. I do not mean to imply the direct influence of *Lazarillo de Tormes*. While Teresa may have been familiar with folkloric trickster tales, it is unlikely that she had read the 1554 masterpiece. Nonetheless, "picaresque" seems an appropriate description: Teresa, at odds against a collection of inept bureaucrats, waffling ecclesiastics and petty landlords, outwits hierarchical authority with ingenuity and determination. Her self-directed humor, while deflating any possible preten-

[8] Jerónimo Gracián de la Madre de Dios, *Obras*, ed. Silverio de Santa Teresa, vols. 15–17 of Biblioteca mística carmelitana (Burgos: El Monte Carmelo, 1933), 16: 202.

tiousness, also serves to diminish the seriousness of her individual acts of disobedience. Traditionally the picaro's self-exposure is a defensive tactic, for he proves that if he is no better than his neighbor, his neighbor is no better than he. A certain amount of deception is a necessary survival tactic in an imperfect world of rogues and fools. Teresa's ecclesiastical "delinquency" is similarly justified. Her picaresque humor—her willingness to set up her own trials as a target for irony—is disarming. As a woman she could not assume a heroic role in her epic of reform. The alternative was to be a pícara, an antiheroine in a mock epic.

EXEMPLARY HISTORY

But *The Book of Foundations*, for all its humor, is not entirely picaresque. After all, Teresa is implicated in two conflicting roles in the reform: as protagonist of the reform her role is to subvert; as its historian her role is to consolidate the new order. Like a usurper who wishes to preserve the principle of hereditary monarchy after a triumphant rebellion, Teresa must find a narrative strategy that will legitimate the disobedience and deception she practiced without undermining the value of absolute obedience to authority that she wished to inculcate in the nuns. In the early chapters advice to prioresses of a decidedly authoritarian cast is interspersed with history. In fact, the anecdotes of exemplary obedience are so extreme as to seem ludicrous to a modern sensibility. In Chapter 1 Teresa tells of testing a nun at the Convent of St. Joseph's in Avila:

> [E]stando un día en refitorio, diéronnos raciones de cogombro; a mí cupo una muy delgada y por de dentro podrida. Llamé con disimulación a una hermana de las de mejor entendimiento y talentos que allí havía, para provar su obediencia, y díjela que fuese a sembrar aquel cogombro a un hortecillo que teníamos. Ella me preguntó si le havía de poner alto u tendido; yo le dije que tendido. Ella fue y pú-

sole, sin venir a su pensamiento que era imposible dejarse de secar, sino que el ser por obediencia le cegó la razón natural para creer era muy acertado. (p. 499)

One day, in the refectory, they gave us portions of cucumber, and mine was a very small one and rotten inside. I called a sister quietly—one of the most intelligent and gifted we had—and, in order to test her obedience, told her to go to her little garden—we each had a garden—and plant the cucumber there. She asked me if she was to plant it upright or sideways. I told her sideways. So she went and planted it, without its ever occurring to her that it could not possibly do anything but shrivel up. The fact that she was acting under obedience blinded her natural reason and made her believe that she was doing quite a normal thing.

(Peers, CW, 3: 2)

It is difficult to reconcile the attitude expressed here—Teresa's admiration for an obedience that blinds natural reason—with the independence and even defiance she showed earlier in the face of opposition to her confessors and the provincial of the entire order. It suggests a psychological "undoing," which replaces the rebelliousness of picaresque wit with a submissive intelligence.

The Book of Foundations, written as it was over a period of nine years, also reveals Teresa in the process of revising and articulating her views on the inevitable conflicts between individual and group that are implicated in conventual life. What was the proper balance between the active and the contemplative life, between mortification and comfort, pain and health? Her celebrated phrase "entre los pucheros anda el Señor" (ch. 5, p. 509) 'the Lord walks among the pots and pans' (Peers, CW, 3: 22) is a recognition of the fact that the economic situation of the early convents and the temperament of some nuns would not permit the intense dedication to the contemplative life she had originally envisioned.[9]

[9] Gracián attributes a similar, if less quotable, sentiment to another Dis-

In addition, Teresa is now much more wary of individual religious practices that might attract the attention of the Inquisition. She writes in Chapter 6 of having to intervene in the case of two nuns who became convinced that they would die if they did not take Communion every day. Teresa persuaded their confessors that this was not a case of ardent piety but "*flaqueza*" or weakness. Initially humoring the two women, she refused to take Communion herself so that the three "could all die together." After a few days the women's morbid convictions abated. The subject of frequent Communion obviously was one that generated inner conflict in Teresa. She had written in her *Life* of her great distress when she was prohibited from communicating frequently, and her most devastating indictment of her father, as we have seen, involved his refusal to allow her to receive the Host when she was near death. Yet by the 1570s eucharistic enthusiasm (the desire to receive many forms or communicate daily) was a suspect Illuminist practice, probably because it was associated with the ecstatic raptures some women experienced while receiving the Host.[10] By 1573 Teresa was much closer to the Church hierarchy on this issue, as she warned her readers: "[C]uando fuere con alguna alteración u pasión y tentándose con la perlada u con el confesor, crean que es conocida tentación [querer confesar], u que si alguno se determina, aunque le diga el confesor que no comulgue, a comulgar" (ch. 6, p. 516) 'If we show any signs of trouble

---

calced prioress. When a novice began to experience ecstatic trances, thus neglecting her duties, the prioress told her: "Sister, here we have no need of your ecstasies; we need someone who can wash the dishes well" (ibid., 17: 191–192).

[10] Hernando de Castillo includes in his list of heretical Illuminist beliefs: "Receiving holy communion with rage and fury as happens here, being discontented and upset and traveling leagues to receive communion when the local priest denies it, is a diabolical furor [furor endemoniado] and not devotion, because true devotion makes men timid, obedient and humble, rather than bent on their own pleasure . . ." (Alvaro Huerga, *Historia de los alumbrados, 1570–1630*, 3 vols. [Madrid: Fundación Universitaria española, 1978], 1: 386).

or passion, or argue with our prioress or our confessor, or if someone decides to communicate even though the confessor forbids it, we may be sure that this desire is a manifest temptation' (my translation).

The Book of Foundations reflects a much more cautious attitude toward supernatural phenomena of all types, reinforced, perhaps, by a partial internalization of the view that women are especially susceptible to delusion: "[E]l natural de las mujeres es flaco, y el amor propio que reina en nosotras muy sutil" (ch. 4, p. 506) 'For women have weak constitutions and the love of self that reins in us is very subtle' (Peers, *CW*, 3: 16). In contrast to the often bold apologia for *arrobamiento*, or rapture, that we find in her first two books, Teresa now begins to entertain the possibility that some nuns might indeed be deluded in their ecstatic experiences. Referring to a Cistercian nun, Teresa writes:

> Estava una monja que no era menos virtuosa que las dichas. Esta con muchas disciplinas y ayunos vino a tanta flaqueza, que cada vez que comulgava u havía ocasión en encenderse en devoción, luego era caída en el suelo y ansí se estava ocho o nueve horas, pareciendo a ella y a todas era arrobamiento. . . . Andava por todo el lugar la fama de los arrobamientos: a mí me pesava de oírlo, porque quiso el Señor entendiese lo que era, y temía en lo que havía de parar. . . . Yo le dije [a su confesor] lo que entendía y cómo era perder tiempo y imposible ser arrobamiento sino flaqueza; que la quitase los ayunos y disciplinas y la hiciese divertir. Ella era obediente; hízolo ansí. Desde a poco que fue tomando fuerza no havía memoria de arrobamiento.   (ch. 6, p. 514)

There was a nun who was not less virtuous than those I have referred to. By dint of much discipline and fasting she had become so weak that, whenever she communicated or had occasion to be enkindled in devotion, she would fall to the ground and remain there for eight or nine hours: both she and the other nuns thought it was a case of rapture. . . . The fame of her raptures spread through the whole town: for

myself, I was sorry to hear of this, for the Lord was pleased
to reveal to me what the matter was and I had misgivings as
to what might come of it. Her confessor, who was a great
friend of mine, came to tell me about it. I gave him my opinion—that she was wasting her time, for these fits could not
possibly be raptures or anything else but the result of weakness. I told him he must forbid her fasting and discipline and
provide her with some distraction. She was obedient and did
as he said. Soon she became stronger and stopped thinking
about raptures.   (Peers, CW, 3: 31–32)

In the *Moradas* Teresa comes up with a derisive neologism
for these trances: "[E]n su seso les parece arrobamiento. Y
llámole yo abovamiento que no es otra cosa más de estar
perdiendo tiempo allí y gastando su salud" (4 *morada*, ch.
3, pp. 371–372) 'They get it into their heads that it is *arrobamiento*, or rapture. But I call it *abobamiento*, foolishness;
for they are doing nothing but wasting their time at it and
ruining their health' (Peers, *CW*, 2: 245–246).[11] If she had
previously dismantled monolithic, binding concepts such
as "humility" and "obedience" into "true" and "false"
components, she now submits "ecstasy" and "union" to
the same procedure, in a way that reinforces the semantic
integrity of "obedience:" "[Q]ue mientra más caváremos
[en la mina de la obedienca], hallaremos más, y mientra
más nos sujetáremos a los hombres, no tiniendo otra voluntad sino la de nuestros mayores, más estaremos seño-
res de ella para conformarla con la de Dios. . . . Esta es la
unión que yo deseo y querría en todas, que no unos em-
bevecimientos muy regalados que hay, a quien tienen
puesto nombre de unión" (ch. 5, pp. 510–511) 'The more
we dig in the mine of obedience, the more we will dis-
cover; and the more we subject ourselves to men, having
no other will but that of our superiors, the more we will
be masters of our will in order to bring it into conformity
with God's. This is the union I desire for all of you, and

[11] The play on words depends on the acoustic similarity of "arrobo"
(trance) and "bobo" (simpleton).

not certain dainty delights, which are sometimes called union' (my translation).

In short, Teresa is now more inclined to admit to the danger of an illusory ecstatic experience, although, significantly, her explanation for it is not supernatural but rather physiological. In the face of an outbreak of *arrobamiento* in the convents Teresa begins to develop her theory that nuns like the ones just described were ill—they were suffering from melancholy, a disease whose symptoms included weeping, scruples (unrealistic remorse), hallucinated visions, locutions, and raptures. The attribution of raptures and visions to melancholy was not original (it can be traced back as far as Aristotle). Teresa's originality lies in her ability to use the theory as a defensive weapon—as a means of protecting her nuns from charges of demonic possession.[12]

In the sixteenth century melancholy referred both to a relatively normal, innate constitution and to a pathological condition, which resulted from an excess of noxious humors. It was believed that melancholy adust, or black bile and its vapors, produced disturbances in perception and reasoning. But although melancholy affected the mind and the emotions, it was considered primarily as a bodily illness.[13] As we can see from the description of the Cister-

[12] The association of melancholy with spiritual exaltation is documented in *Problem XXX*, attributed to Aristotle (Raymond Klibansky, Erwin Panofsky, and Fritz Saxl, *Saturn and Melancholy: Studies in the History of Natural Philosophy, Religion, and Art* [London: Nelson, 1964], p. 24). Girolamo Fracastoro (*Opera Omnia*, 1555) and Rhazes (*Continens*, 1529) also described raptures and beatific visions as melancholy symptoms (Lawrence Babb, *The Elizabethan Malady: A Study of Melancholia in English Literature from 1580 to 1642* [East Lansing: Michigan State College Press, 1951], p. 48). It is difficult to determine the immediate sources for Teresa's ideas on melancholy; since she did not read Latin, she could have not had direct knowledge of Fracastoro and Rhazes. In sixteenth-century Spain, however, medicine was a *converso* profession; therefore her knowledge may have derived from personal, family contacts. Personal contacts with Jesuits is another possibility.

[13] For a survey of Renaissance ideas on melancholy see Babb, *The Elizabethan Malady*. Almost all writers on melancholy distinguished sadness

cian nun, Teresa identified the precipitating factor for convent melancholy as excessive asceticism.[14] Teresa's definition of nuns' melancholy is, of course, notably different
from that of an antipapist like Robert Burton, whose *Anatomy of Melancholy* condemned "Popish Monasteries" for
binding men and women "to lead a single life against the
laws of nature."[15] In Teresa's conception, over-zealous
fasting, vigils, and penance simply weaken the body, allowing atrabilious vapors to affect the brain.

Having identified the etiology of the disease, Teresa first
recommends a therapy designed to eliminate the debilitat-
ing practices and strengthen the body: improved diet
(more meat, less fish), rest, and oral rather than mental
prayer. She also advocates an emotionally supportive environment; one shouldn't distress the melancholics by telling them that their visions come from the devil. One must
listen to them as sick persons, even humor them: "Las
prioras han menester, sin que las mesmas lo entiendan,
llevarlas con mucha piadad, ansí como verdadera madre,

caused by misfortunes or the death of loved ones from pathological melancholy.

[14] Doctor Huarte de San Juan, in his enormously influential *Examen de
ingenios* (1575), also attributed preternatural sensations to certain ascetic
practices. Specifically he offered a humoral explanation for the tactile in-
sensibility experienced during meditation (Huerga, *Historia de los alumbrados*, 2: 361). Similarly, Robert Burton, in *Anatomy of Melancholy* (1621), described "religious melancholy" as follows: "Never any strange illusions
of devils amongst hermits, Anchorites, never any visions, phantasms,
apparitions, enthusiasms, Prophets, any revelations, but immoderate
fasting, bad diet, sickness, melancholy, solitariness, or some such things
were the precedent causes, the forerunners or concomitants of them" (3:
393, quoted in Babb, *The Elizabethan Malady*, p. 49).

[15] Quoted in Ilza Veith, *Hysteria: The History of a Disease* (Chicago: University of Chicago Press, 1965), p. 129. Although Burton sees a relationship between sexual abstinence and melancholy, in general, hysteria and
melancholy did not merge in medical theory until the end of the seventeenth century (Babb, *The Elizabethan Malady*, p. 28). I believe Marco Merenciano exaggerates the similarity between Teresian melancholy and
Freudian notions of hysteria precisely because Teresa ignored the possibility of a sexual etiology for the disease (Francisco Marco Merenciano,
Ensayos médicos y literarios [Madrid: Editorial Cultura hispánica, 1958]).

y buscar los medios que pudiera para su remedio" (ch. 7, p. 518) 'Without their realizing it, prioresses must treat these nuns very kindly, like true mothers, and seek possible means of curing them' (Peers, CW, 3: 39). Although Teresa recommends compassionate tolerance for nuns whose reason has been affected by their disease, she recognizes different degrees of melancholic affliction, ranging from slight disorders in reason to a condition approaching madness. The degree of culpability is then inversely proportional to the severity of the disease; when the melancholy humors dominate the reason, there is no more question of culpability than there would be in madmen. But for those whose reason is only "sickly" a certain degree of culpability remains (ch. 7, p. 517). Teresa is thus quite adamant that the same standards of docility and obedience to authority apply, regardless of the severity of the affliction: "Si la que es melancólica resistiere al perlado, que lo pague como la sana y ninguna cosa se le perdone" (ch. 7, p. 518) 'If a melancholy nun should resist her superior, she must on no account be excused but must pay for it as a nun would who was well' (Peers, CW, 3: 38).[16] "Si no bastaren palabras, sean castigos; si no bastaren pequeños, sean grandes; si no bastare un mes de tenerlas encarceladas, sean cuatro, que no pueden hacer mayor bien a sus almas" (ch. 7, p. 517) 'If words do not suffice, they must be punished; if trifling punishments are not sufficient, they must have severe ones; if one month's imprisonment is not sufficient, they must have four: there is no better way of benefiting their souls' (Peers, CW, 3: 37).

---

[16] Later she would write in her *Method for the Visitation of Convents*: "A éstas es menester no mostrar blandura, porque si con algo piensan salir, jamás cesarán de inquietar ni se sosegarán, sino que entiendan siempre que han de ser castigadas y que para esto [el visitador] ha de favorcer a la perlada" (*Visita de descalzas*, p. 628) 'With melancholy nuns, he [the examining priest] must never be gentle, for if [melancholy nuns] think they can get their own way about anything, they will never cease giving trouble and settle down quietly. So they must always realize that they are liable to be punished; and for this reason the vistor must take the side of the prioress (Peers, CW, 3: 243).

Teresa again resorts to the analogy between melancholy and madness, but this time, paradoxically, it is used to justify the "hard line" for melancholics:

> Parece sin justicia que si no puede más castiguen a la enferma como a la sana. Luego también lo sería atar a los locos y azotarlos, sino dejarlos matar a todos. Créanme, que lo he provado, y que, a mi parecer, intentado hartos remedios, que no hallo otro. Y la priora que por piadad dejare comenzar a tener libertad a las tales, en fin fin [sic] no se podrá sufrir, y cuando se venga a remediar, será haviendo hecho mucho daño a las otras.   (ch. 7, p. 518)

It seems unjust to punish one who is sick like one who is well when the former cannot help herself. But it seems equally so to bind and chastise madmen instead of allowing them to kill everybody. Believe me, I have tried both ways, and I think I have attempted every kind of remedy, and there is none but this. A prioress who out of the kindness of her heart has begun to allow such nuns freedom will eventually find it impossible to do anything with them, and there will be no curing them until great harm has been done to the rest.   (Peers, CW, 3: 38).

Teresa's use of the word "freedom" is initially confusing; she is not warning against lax behavior but the freedom to engage in forbidden asceticism or irregular devotional practices—such as over-frequent Communion—that might continue to induce the questionable trances. The afflicted must submit in all humility to the devotional limitations imposed by their prioresses: "Mas torno a decir que las que no hicieren esto de grado, que sean apremiadas de las perladas y no se engañen con piadades indiscretas, para que se vengan a alborotar todas con sus desconciertos" (ch. 7, p. 518) 'I repeat that those who do not willingly act in this way must be disciplined by their superiors and must not deceive themselves with indiscreet shows of piety lest they upset all the other sisters by their exaggerations' (Peers, CW, 3: 38). Bearing this in mind, it is easier to understand Teresa's ambivalence toward melancholy nuns. On the one hand, she admired ascetic fervor; on the other hand, she saw melancholy as a vicious cycle of excessive asceticism that weakened the body and the mind, thereby inciting its victims to perform further acts of extreme piety, often in disobedience of their superiors.

It is this conception of melancholy as a disease of disobedience that allows Teresa to make a concession to demonology—she allows that the devil takes advantage of vulnerable individuals to provoke dissent, factionalism, and insubordination within the convent. In *The Book of Her Life* Teresa had energetically dismissed the demonological fears of her confessors to the extent that these fears are seen as more harmful than the devil himself: "¡[U]na higa para todos los demonios! que ellos temerán a mí. No entiendo estos miedos: ¡demonio, demonio!, adonde podemos decir ¡Dios, Dios! y hacerle temblar. . . . Es sin duda que tengo ya más miedo a los que tan grande le tienen a el demonio que a él mesmo; porque él no me puede hacer nada, y estotros, en especial si son confesores, inquietan mucho" (*Vida*, Ch. 25, p. 104) 'A fig for the devils, because they shall fear me. I don't understand these fears, "The devil, the devil!" when we can say "God! God!" and make the devil tremble. . . . Without doubt, I fear those who have such great fear of the devil more than I do the devil himself, for he can't do anything to me. Whereas these others, especially if they are confessors, cause severe disturbance.'[17] In *Foundations* the best protection against the devil is *obedience* to confessors: "[Y]endo con limpia conciencia y con obediencia, nunca el Señor primite que el demonio tenga tanta mano que nos engañe de manera que pueda dañar el alma" (ch. 4, p. 506) 'If we walk with a pure conscience and in obedience, the Lord will never al-

[17] *The Book of Her Life*, trans. Kieran Kavanaugh and Otilo Rodríguez, vol. 1 of *The Collected Works of St. Teresa of Avila* (Washington, D.C.: Institute of Carmelite Studies, 1976), 1: 170.

low the devil to have such power over us as to deceive us in a way that can harm our souls' (Peers, *CW*, 3: 16). Although the devil appears to be more persistent and troublesome in *Foundations*, we should recognize that, in comparison with the demonological theories brought to bear on the Illuminists, the powers of Teresa's devil are quite limited.[18]

Although Teresa's conception of melancholy is grounded in the physiological, she does consider the possibility of a behavioral variation. She recognized that the century's favorite malady could spread very quickly in a convent: "Porque hay otro daño grandísimo, . . . : que como la ven [a la melancólica], a su parecer, buena, como no entienden la fuerza que le hace el mal en lo interior, es tan miserable nuestro natural que cada una le parecerá es melancólica para que la sufran" (ch. 7, p. 518) 'In addition to the danger which has already been described, there is another and a very great one. So miserable is our nature that, when a person suffering in this way shows every sign of being in good health, all her companions, having no idea of the seriousness of her inward malady, will think that they too are afflicted by melancholy, and that their little ways may be put up with too' (Peers, *CW*, 3: 38). Nonetheless, Teresa never really developed this line of observation and I think realized the difficulty of separating melancholics and their mimics into discrete groups.[19] For

[18] Also see her remarks in *Las moradas del castillo interior* (4 *morada*, ch. 3) and *Camino de perfección* (Escorial codex, ch. 5). Teresa's theories are not dissimilar to those of the witchcraft dissenter Johann Weyer whose 1563 *De Praestigiis* rejected the idea of carnal copulation between women in devils while allowing that melancholics were especially susceptible to demonic interference (Sydney Anglo, "Melancholy and Witchcraft: The Debate between Wier, Bodin, and Scot," in *Folie et déraison à la Renaissance* [Brussels: Editions de la Université de Bruxelles, 1976], pp. 209–222 at 213). Even Burton believed that the devil finds the melancholy easy prey (Babb, *The Elizabethan Malady*, p. 49).

[19] In this respect Teresa's ideas are closer to those of an anti-Freudian, Thomas Szasz (*The Myth of Mental Illness* [1961; reprint ed., New York: Harper and Row, 1974]), who views hysteria as the semiconscious mimicry of organic disease. López Ibor observes that Teresa did not make a

all its emphasis on the organic, on the noxious black fumes that clouded the brain, melancholy was a concept that tended to spill over the borders of the mind/body dichotomy. Physiopathology overlapped at some undefinable point with sociopathology; melancholy was a physical disease that induced insubordination, a disease that weakened an nun's resistance to, without absolving her from, the sins of pride and disobedience.

When it comes to the subject of visions, Teresa also seems to be moving closer to the Counter-Reformation line. She again avers that congenital weakness makes women susceptible to false visions: "Téngase aviso que la flaqueza natural es muy flaca, en especial en las mujeres— y en este camino de oración se muestra más—, y ansí es menester que a cada cosita que se nos antoje, no pensemos luego es cosa de visión" (ch. 8, p. 520) 'It should be remembered that the weakness of our nature is very great, especially in women, and that it shows itself most markedly in this way of prayer; so it is essential that we should not at once suppose every little imagining of ours to be a vision' (Peers, CW, 3: 43). She is especially distrustful of prophetic visions, which she considered highly dangerous, and warns again that in such cases nuns submit in complete obedience to the opinion of their confessor (ch. 8).

Although Teresa was, after 1573, much more inclined to doubt the signs of ecstasy, her new position could be seen as a strategic—even paradoxically subversive—retreat rather than a complete capitulation. As much as her repeated references to women's "flaqueza" suggest an internalization of prevailing misogynistic views, we should note that in most cases Teresa presents women's weakness as primarily physiological rather than moral or spiritual; women are physically disadvantaged in their pursuit of

---

strict distinction between the attitudinal and the pathological components of melancholy (Juan José López Ibor, "Ideas de Santa Teresa sobre la melancholía," *Revista de espiritualidad* 22 [1963]: 423–443 at p. 433).

perfection, but they are never spiritually disqualified.[20] Consistent with her former views, she continues to dismiss alarm over diabolical influence as largely unwarranted. False visions are more likely to come from "our imagination and bad humors" than from the devil. At a time when certain theologians considered ecstatic visions to be the result of carnal intercourse with the devil, Teresa steered a middle course between a physiological and a supernatural etiology of visions and raptures. Although she allowed that the devil might "take advantage" of a melancholy humor, producing false visions, voices, and prophecies, she ignored the sexual phobias implicit in the diabolical theory of ecstasy and simply advised the nuns to resist the visions, to reveal all to one's confessor, and never to act on commands received through visions without permission from a confessor. She continued to believe in the possibility of authentic, divinely inspired ecstasy, although she attempted to deemphasize its significance in the pursuit of perfection: "En lo que está la suma perfeción claro está que no es en regalos interiores ni en grandes arrobamientos ni visiones ni en espíritu de profecía, sino en estar nuestra voluntad . . . conforme con la de Dios" (ch. 5, p. 510) 'The highest perfection consists not in interior favours or in great raptures or in visions or in the spirit of prophecy, but in the bringing of our wills . . . into conformity with the will of God' (Peers, CW, 3: 23). But she also came to believe in the existence of a self-induced pathological ecstasy. Teresa knew that when a nun experienced the trance, her body became a text of portentous and ambiguous signs that could attract not only the adulation of a populace hungry for saints and miracles but also the projective sexual fantasies of the demonologists. By deemphasizing and demystifying *arrobamiento*, Teresa

---

[20] Dominique Deneuville argues that Teresa's pessimism about human character in general increases with age and that in later years her pejorative references to female *"flaqueza"* are matched by equally pejorative estimation of male character weaknesses (*Santa Teresa de Jesús y la mujer,* trans. Fernando Gutiérrez [Barcelona: Herder, 1966], pp. 117–124).

sought to protect her nuns from the fate of a Magdalena de la Cruz. But by insisting on their complete submission to their superiors, she was retreating from ground that she had previously won for herself.[21] Teresa's warnings against excessive penance and devotion are, however, interspersed with stories of nuns, like Beatriz de la Encarnación, who practiced extreme mortification. Moved with pity for prisoners of the Inquisition who had been condemned to death, Beatriz prayed to suffer for their sins. She was rewarded with a continuous high fever and an intestinal abscess. With obvious admiration, Teresa writes, "En cosas de mortificación era estremada. Con una disimulación se apartava de cualquiera cosa que fuese de recreación, que, si no era quien andava sobre aviso, no le entendían. No parecía que vivía ni tratava con las criaturas—según se le dava poco de todo" (ch. 12, pp. 529–530) 'In matters of mortification she was austere in the extreme. She was so clever at withdrawing secretly from every kind of recreation that only those who were watching her closely would realize what she was doing. She seemed not to be living or having any intercourse with creatures at all, so little store did she set by any of them' (Peers, CW, 3: 59). Also curious is Teresa's attitude toward the rigorous discipline practiced at the Discalced monastery at Duruelo, where John of the Cross was a founding member. Although she writes that she chastised the monks for their excessive penance and warned them

---

[21] In a veiled autobiographical reference in Las moradas del castillo interior Teresa complains of a confessor who tormented his spiritual daughter by attributing her supernatural favors to "the devil or melancholy." Nonetheless, she adds in a way that reveals her present concern over the phenomenon, "Y de ésta está el mundo tan lleno, que no me espanto; que hay tanta ahora en el mundo y hace el demonio tantos males por este camino, que tienen muy mucha razón de temerlo y mirarlo muy bien los confesores" 'And the world is so full of it [melancholy] that this is no surprise to me; for there's so much of it about now, and the devil takes so much advantage of it, that confessors have very good reason to be afraid of it and look into it carefully' (6 morada, ch. 1, p. 387, my translation).

that they might be playing into the devil's hands, she confesses that she was relieved that they ignored her advice (ch. 14).

REBEL DAUGHTERS: HISTORY AS NOVELLA

Given the attraction of authority in *The Book of Foundation's*, several narratives of girls who ran away from home to join the convent are particularly arresting. Some of them are treated with much imaginative detail and, like intercalated *novelle*, have narrative unity of their own. Remembering Teresa's own history as a runaway daughter, we can understand her fascination with these stories as imaginative rewritings of her own life.

The first case history of a runaway tells of Casilda de Padilla, the only remaining heir of her noble family's fortune. So anxious were her relatives to keep the fortune in the family that she was betrothed to her uncle at the age of eleven. At first Casilda enjoyed the luxuries of her station, and even grew to love her fiancé-uncle. However, a visit to the Carmelite convent in Valladolid convinced her that her salvation depended on her marriage to Christ. Teresa concisely conjures up the series of dramatic scenes precipitated by Casilda's change of heart. Her obstinacy clearly put everyone in a compromising position. Her mother, though supposedly very pious, feared offending her relatives if the girl's engagement were broken. The prioress feared charges of undue influence, and the confessors were reluctant to oppose the wishes of a powerful family. It took an entire day to persuade the girl to leave the convent. Later, on a carriage ride Casilda ordered her servants to stop by the convent with a gift of firewood. When the door was opened, she slipped in and once more refused to leave. The pleas of her beloved uncle were to no avail. Eventually her relatives obtained a royal order and had her forcibly removed from the convent. Undaunted, Casilda made a third attempt and was finally successful. Teresa describes the incident with inventive detail:

Y ansí, un día, yendo a misa con su madre, estando en la iglesia, entróse su madre a confesar en un confisionario, y ella rogó a su aya que fuese a uno de los padres a pedir que le dijesen una misa. Y en viéndola ida, metió sus chapines en la manga y alzó la saya, y vase con la mayor priesa que pudo a este monesterio, que era harto lejos. Su aya, como no la halló, fuése tras ella; y ya que llegava cerca, rogó a un hombre que se la tuviese. El dijo después que no havía podido menearse, a ansí, la dejó. Ella, como entró a la puerta del monesterio primera, y cerró la puerta y comenzó a llamar. Cuando llegó la aya, ya estava dentro en el monesterio, y diéronle luego el hábito.   (ch. 11, p. 528)

So one day, when she was in a church, where she had gone with her mother to hear Mass, and her mother went to a confessional to make her confession, she asked her governess to go to one of the Fathers and beg him to say a Mass for her. When she saw that she had gone, she stuck her overshoes up her sleeves, caught up her skirt and [runs] with the greatest possible haste to this convent, which was a long way away. Her governess, not finding her, went after her, and, as she was approaching the convent, called to a man to stop her. Later the man said he had found himself unable to stir, and so had let her go. The girl entered by the outer door of the convent, shut it behind her and began to cry out. By the time her governess arrived, she was already in the convent, where they gave her the habit at once.

(Peers, CW, 3: 56)

From a theological standpoint there is no inconsistency here. Casilda, convinced of her vocation, was simply obedient to a higher authority than her family. Politically, the issue was a sensitive one and could hardly be expected to improve relations between the Carmelites and the lay community. It is not surprising that Casilda's story was suppressed when *The Book of Foundations* was first pub-

lished in 1610. But what is telling is Teresa's interest in the
drama of conflicting loyalties, her suspenseful rendering
of Casilda's escape (with an excited shift to the present
tense), and her attention to the narrative details of the episode. We might wonder, in fact, if some details—Casilda
taking off her shoes to run faster—are not purely novelis-
tic. Teresa was obviously fascinated with this story of adolescent rebellion and willing to take some risks in the telling of it.

The story of Catalina Godínez, patroness of the Convent
of Beas, offers another case of parent-child conflict. Catalina was also heir to her family's fortune, and at the age of
fourteen vigorously resisted her parents' plans to arrange
a marriage for her. She put on humble clothing, unbefit-
ting her rank, and exposed her face to the sun to make
herself unattractive to suitors. After five years of continued parental opposition and ill health, she took the Carmelite veil. Teresa writes that once she was a nun, her obedience was complete. She became quite detached from her
relatives and was always anxious to be sent far away from
her home. Her greatest pleasure was to be treated harshly
(ch. 22).

The story of Beatriz de Chávez (later Beatriz de la Madre
de Dios) is perhaps the most pathetic. At the age of seven
she was sent by her parents to live with a childless aunt.
Three friends of the aunt who had hoped to inherit her
fortune, seeing that the girl was likely to displace them,
concocted the story that the little girl was planning to poi-
son her aunt. Both Beatriz's aunt and mother believed the
slanderous accusations, and the girl was sent home where
she was beaten, tortured, and made to sleep on the floor
for a year. Beatriz refused to confess the crime, and her
mother became even more hardened against her. When
she reached a marriageable age, her parents where anxious to find a husband for her, since she was the only sur-
viving child, though "the one whom they loved least." But
Beatriz informed them that she had made a vow never to
marry, not even if they killed her. Predictably her parents

assumed she refused to marry because she had committed some evil deed. They beat her, tried to strangle her, and, Teresa writes, it was only with luck that she wasn't killed. As a result of this mistreatment she was confined to bed for three months. Yet Teresa appears to be sympathetic toward the mother, whom she describes as a virtuous, truthful, and a most Christian woman. The father is also described favorably as "a most sensible man." Teresa appears to attribute the conflict between Beatriz and her parents to supernatural causes—benevolent as well as malevolent: "El demonio que los cegava, u Dios que lo primitía, para que ésta fuese mártir . . ." (ch. 26, p. 572) 'Either through blindness sent them by the devil or by the permission of God so that she should be a martyr . . .' (Peers, *CW*, 3: 136); "A quien nuestro Señor quiere hacer mercedes de que padezca, tiene muchos medios" (Ch 26, p. 572) 'But when Our Lord wishes to grant anyone the grace to suffer, He has many ways of doing so' (Peers, *CW*, 3: 137). At the age of twenty-seven Beatriz evaded her chaperon and stole away to the Discalced convent in Seville. Like Casilda and Catalina before her, Beatriz cheerfully submitted to the discipline of the convent: "[T]an humilde y amiga [era] de hacer cuanto havía, que teníamos harto que hacer en quitarle la escoba" (ch. 26, p. 573) 'She was so humble and so fond of doing anything there was to be done that we found it difficult to take the broom from her' (Peers, *CW*, 3: 139). According to Teresa's account, Beatriz was so happy as a nun that she grew quite plump. Her mother eventually reconciled herself to her daughter's vocation and in fact entered the same convent after her husband's death, and bequeathed all her possessions to it. Teresa concludes by reporting that mother and daughter were living together "con grandísimo contento" 'in the greatest of happiness.' In spite of the mother's apparent remorse, given the appalling account of the child's torture, Teresa's refusal to condemn the mother, coupled with the decision to allow her to become a Carmelite, is definitely a disconcerting resolution to the story.

Even more perplexing is the fact that the protagonist of this exemplary narrative was one of the two rebel nuns in the Seville convent who later denounced Teresa to the Inquisition. From Teresa's letters we learn that once inside the convent walls Beatriz became a notorious troublemaker. She grew excessively fond of her confessor: Teresa complained that the confessor "la tenía sorbido el seso"[22] 'had sucked her brains dry.' Beatriz and another nun, Isabel de San Jerónimo, began to have visions and revelations. In her letter of October 23, 1576, Teresa confided to Gracián her growing ambivalence about the nuns' stability:

> De la San Jerónimo, será menester hacerla comer carne algunos días y quitarla la oración y mandarla vuestra paternidad que no trate sino con él, u que me escriva, que tiene flaca la imaginación y lo que medita le parece que ve y oye; bien que algunas veces será verdad y lo ha sido, que es muy buena alma.
>
> De Beatriz me parece lo mesmo, aunque eso que me escriven del tiempo de la profesión no me parece antojo sino harto bien; ha menester ayunar poco. Mándelo vuestra paternidad a la priora, y que no las deje tener oración a tiempos sino ocupadas en otros oficios, porque no vengamos a mal, y créame que es menester esto.   (*Cartas*, p. 773)

As for (Isabel de) San Jerónimo, she will have to be made to eat meat for a few days, and to give up prayer, and your Paternity must order her to have no communication with anyone but yourself, or, in writing, with me. For she has an unsteady imagination which leads her to think she is seeing and hearing the things she meditates upon. At the same time, she may occasionally be right, as she has sometimes been in the past, for she is a very good soul.

The same, I think is true of Beatriz, though what they tell me happened at the time of her profession seems to be no fancy but a wonderful favour. She must fast very little. Tell

---

[22] Llamas, *Santa Teresa*, p. 153.

the Prioress not to allow them to be at prayer all the time, but to keep them busy with other offices lest we find worse things happening. Believe me, this is really necessary.[23]

However, when in imitation of the mother foundress, the nuns began to record their visions, Teresa became genuinely alarmed. On March 28, 1578, she wrote the Seville prioress, María de San José:

[N]o estoy bien en que esas hermanas escrivan las cosas de oración, porque hay muchos inconvenientes que quisiera decirlos. Sepa que aunque no sea sino gastar tiempo y que es estorbo para andar el alma con libertad, y aun se pueden figurar hartas cosas. . . . Si son cosas de tomo, nunca se olvidan; y si se olvidan, ya no hay para qué las decir.

(*Cartas*, p. 869)

I do not approve of your nuns' writing on subjects to do with prayer; there are many disadvantages in the practice which I should like to mention. You must realize that it is not only a waste of time; it interferes with the soul's freedom of action; and then, too, it may lead the nuns to imagine all kinds of things. . . . If their experiences are of any substance, they will never forget them; and if they are of a kind that can be forgotten, there is no point in their writing them down.

(Peers, *Letters*, 2: 544).

She goes on to recommend that they be given meat and have their prayer restricted. Undaunted, the two nuns claimed the gift of prophecy; they practiced extreme mortification and began to demand frequent confession and long conversations with their confessor. When the prioress sought to limit this contact, Beatriz and another nun denounced Teresa, the prioress, and Gracián to the Inquisition. Although the original accusations have disappeared, we know from other reports and the subsequent

[23] *The Letters of Saint Teresa of Jesus*, trans. E. Allison Peers, 2 vols. (London: Burns, Oates and Washbourne, 1951), 1: 318; hereafter abbreviated as Peers, *Letters*.

retractions that Gracián was accused of sleeping in the
convent, of changing his clothes there, of having embraced and kissed the nuns, and of having danced naked
before them. Teresa and Gracián were also accused of having illicit relations. The Inquisition refused to act on the
accusations, the charges were dismissed, and, more remarkably, the two nuns were reconciled to their community.[24] In a letter written on May 3, 1579, Teresa pleaded
with the convent to forgive and pray for the wayward
nuns. Beatriz in particular seems to be the object of Teresa's compassion: "[Yo] . . . la tenía por engañada y persona de flaca imaginación, aparejada para que le hiciese el
demonio trampantojos como lo ha hecho, que sabe muy
bien aprovecharse del natural y poco entendimiento, y
ansí no hay que la echar tanta culpa, sino haverla gran lástima. . . . Yo la considero como una persona fuera de sí,
en parte. . . . Oración, hermanas, oración por ella, que
también cayeron muchos santos y lo tornaron a ser" (Cartas, pp. 918–920) 'I thought . . . she was merely a weak-
minded person who had been led astray: she was just ripe
to be tricked by the devil, as she has been, for he is very
good at taking advantage of temperamental and unintelli-
gent people. So we must not blame her so much as be very
sorry for her. . . . In some ways I look upon her as a person out of her mind. . . . Pray, sisters, pray for her, for
many of the saints have fallen and then become saints
again' (Peers, Letters, 2: 647–648).

When, in spite of this benevolent treatment, Beatriz refused to retract her accusations, Teresa finally recommended harsh punishment. In a letter to María de San
José, dated July 4, 1580, Teresa writes, "Yo he estado bien
penada . . . cómo la dejavan comulgar. Yo le digo, madre,
que no es razón se queden sin castigo cosas semejantes, y
que la cárcel perpetua que ella dice que estaba ya deter-

[24] For the history of Teresa's problems with the Inquisition in Seville
and the text of Beatriz's retraction, see Llamas, Santa Teresa, pp. 137–219.
Beatriz took the veil in 1576; she denounced Teresa and Gracián to the
Inquisition in 1578. The second nun was Margarita de la Concepción.

minado por acá, que era bien que no saliese de ella" (*Cartas*, p. 974) 'I was very shocked . . . to see they had allowed her to receive Holy Communion. I must say, Mother, it is not right such things (as she has done) should remain unpunished; and she should not have been allowed to leave the continuous confinement which, as you say, we had decided upon' (Peers, *Letters*, 2: 760). Beatriz finally made her retraction at the end of 1580.

It is no wonder that Teresa omitted this painful episode from her history of the Discalced reform. But why, when she returned to the manuscript on three subsequent occasions, did she not strike Beatriz's early story from her history as well?[25] Why does Beatriz remain as the exemplary heroine of the Seville foundation? In fact, we might wonder why Teresa included so many stories of rebellious daughters at a time when Illuminists were accused of fomenting filial disobedience.[26] In a period in which obedience to secular and religious authority was paramount Teresa's narratives could only have been prejudicial to her reform. It is possible that here Teresa's psychological needs outweighed her usual political acumen. While she identified with the young girls' rejection of their parents' authority, she was also made uneasy by the vehemence of their rejection and was anxious to emphasize their docile behavior after their incorporation into the community. The narratives betray not only the continued sympathy Teresa felt for adolescent rebels but a compensatory identification with a parental role. In a sense the foundations were a means by which Teresa attempted to act out contradictory desires simultaneously, rejecting the paternal home and

[25] It seems most probable that Teresa wrote Beatriz's story shortly after November 1577 (the date alluded to when her mother took the veil). From Teresa's October 1576 letter we can see that Beatriz was a cause for concern almost from the time she professed. Teresa added to the *Book of Foundations* in 1579, after the foundations of Soria in 1581, and again after Granada and Burgos in 1582. But on none of these occasions did she alter her account of Beatriz.

[26] Llamas, *Santa Teresa*, p. 114.

atoning for rebellion through submission to a renewed, utopian authority. Each foundation was a search for an environment in which intimacy did not provoke guilt, in which authority could be reconciled with forgiveness. The desire for reconciliation was so compelling that Teresa idealized a denouement for Beatriz and her abusive mother. In Teresa's exemplary *novella* a happy ending belies the psychological damage of Beatriz's past and silences an unhappy epilogue of continued rebellion.

HISTORY AS REPETITION

Again and again Teresa removed herself from the tranquility she had so laboriously constructed. In her activity as foundress she not only reenacted her flight from home, she also repeatedly denied herself the comfort of affectionate ties. Detachment from one's biological family was a prerequisite virtue for the novice, but, as Teresa grudgingly admits, it was frequently replaced with affection for the mother foundress:

> Y en dejar las hijas y hermanas mías, cuando me iva de una parte a otra, yo os digo que, como yo las amo tanto, que no ha sido la más pequeña cruz, en especial cuando pensava que no las havía de tornar a ver y vía su gran sentimiento y lágrimas. Que aunque están [las monjas] de otras desasidas, ésta no se lo ha dado Dios, por ventura para que me fuese a mí más tormento, que tampoco lo estoy de ellas, aunque me esforzava todo lo que podía para no se lo mostrar y las reñía; mas poco me aprovechava, que es grande el amor que me tienen y bien se ve en muchas cosas ser verdadero.
>
> (Epílogo, p. 577)

[Leaving my sisters and daughters when I went from one place to another, since I love them so much, I assure you, was no small cross to bear.] For, though they are detached from everything else, God has not granted them detachment in this, perhaps in order that it may be the greater torment to me. Nor am I detached from them, though I have always done my utmost not to show this, and indeed have rebuked them for their attachment. But this did little good, for their love for me is very deep and there are many ways in which it can be seen how true it is.   (Peers, *CW*, 3: 146)

In *The Book of Her Life* Teresa had also justified emotional detachment. She had used her discourse to protest a psychological as well as a theological double bind. However, as mother foundress she re-creates the binding role of an authoritarian parent, who, like her father, demands both autonomy and obedience, love and detachment. One strand of the double bind is embedded in the picaresque history—the story of how to reject authority. The other strand lies in the exemplary *novelle*, the stories that promise definitive reconciliation through surrender to an ideal authority. This is not to deny historical determinants: monastic life is, after all, predicated upon the twin poles of obedience and detachment from family. But Teresa's creative history points beyond the exigence for institutional order; it suggests to me the vital intertwining of dreams and reality, the poignant convergence of psychological needs and theological constraints. Teresa's persuasiveness, the success of her subversive rhetoric paradoxically won for her partial freedom from a rhetoric of humility. She had successfully defended the primacy of individual experience over institutionalized theology but subsequently found herself in a position to make authoritative pronouncements on orthodoxy in others. As Teresa seeks to institutionalize her antihierarchical spirituality, her discourse reweaves the binding skein.

Conclusion

THE GOLDEN PEN

TERESA had first taken up the pen at the command of her confessors; if she began to write out of apologetic necessity, she continued to write with apostolic zeal, first for an intimate audience of nuns in her reformed order, then for an expanding circle of disciples and admirers. The success of her rhetoric on one reader is reflected in the words of Fray Domingo Báñez in his Approbation for *The Book of Her Life*:

> I have read with great attention this book in which Teresa of Jesus . . . sets down a plain account of all that takes place in her soul, so as to have the instruction and guidance of her confessors. In the whole of it I have found nothing which to my mind is erroneous teaching, while there is much good and edifying counsel for people who engage in prayer. For the great experience of this nun, and the discretion and humility which have always led her to seek enlightenment from her confessors to profit from their learning, enable her to write well concerning prayer, as the most learned men are sometimes unable to do for lack of experience. There is only one thing in this book with which, after it has been fully examined, fault can fairly be found—namely, that it says a great deal about revelations and visions, which are always very much to be feared, especially in women, who are more apt to believe that they come from God. . . . They are to be regarded rather as trials full of peril to those who are striving after perfection, for Satan is wont to transform himself into an angel of light and to delude souls that are curious and lacking in humiility, as we have seen in our own times. Still we must not for this reason lay down a general rule that all these revelations and visions are of the devil. . . .

> This woman, to judge from her report, is not a deceiver, even though she might to some extent be herself deceived, for she speaks so plainly, both of what is good and of what is bad, and is so eager to write to good effect, that she leaves no doubt of the excellence of her intention.[1]

Teresa's rhetoric of feminine subordination—all the paradoxes, the self-depreciation, the feigned ignorance and incompetence, the deliberate obfuscation and ironic humor—produced the desired perlocutionary effect. Her words were taken as an ingenuous act: "This woman is not a deceiver."

The publication of her works by Fray Luis de León in 1588, six years after her death, would appear to confirm, furthermore, that her teachings had finally been accepted within the margins of orthodoxy. But the Spanish Church was still troubled by the plague of *mujercillas*. As the popular Jesuit Pedro de Rivadeneira wrote: "It is indeed lamentable to see the multitude of deceived little women [*mujercillas engañadas*] who have appeared in our day in the most illustrious cities of Spain; women who with their ecstasies, revelations and stigmata have upset and fooled many people."[2] The posthumous debate over Teresa's works in the same year reveals how precarious her success was and how close she came to fulfilling the alternative destiny of a forgotten "visionary nun" hypothesized by Charles Henry Lea.

In 1589, the same year Rivadeneira preached his sermon against *mujercillas*, Alonso de la Fuente, one of the Inquisition's most energetic prosecutors of Illuminists in Extremadura, initiated a campaign to have Teresa's works

[1] "Censura del P. Domingo Báñez en el autógrafo de la *Vida* (1575), in *Obras completas*, edición manual, ed. Efrén de la Madre de Dios and Otger Steggink (Madrid: Católica, 1962), pp. 178–179; translation found in *The Complete Works of Saint Teresa* by E. Allison Peers, 3 vols. (London: Sheed and Ward, 1944–1946), 3: 333–336.
[2] Pedro de Rivadeneira, S. J., "Tratado de la tribulación," in *Obras escogidas*, vol. 60 of Biblioteca de autores españoles (Madrid: Biblioteca de autores españoles, 1899), p. 439.

banned.[3] "Having read and considered the works of Mother Teresa de Jesús attentively, I find in them writings of the Masilian sect with signs of other sects, especially ecstatic heretics, *alumbrados* and *dejados*" (p. 396). Teresa's books, written "principally for women," so avidly bought and read, are likened to a dark wind of a secret and poisonous heresy. Fray Alonso even proposes that Teresa may not be the real author of the books that bear her name, for though they be diabolical, "they exceed the capacity of women" (pp. 396–397).

In five memorials to the Inquisition written between 1589 and 1591 the friar repeats his assertion that Teresa's works are heretical. Teresa's intellectual leadership is taken as prima facie evidence of heterodoxy. Alluding to the primary role of women in Illuminist sects, Alonso writes:

> That learned men should come to learn from a woman and recognize her as a leader in matters of prayer and spiritual doctrine . . . is an argument for the novelty [i.e., heterodoxy] of this doctrine, in which this woman was wise, and the men who subjected themselves to her were foolish; for in the ancient doctrine of the Church educated and learned men knew more than women. But it is nothing new for women of erroneous life and doctrine to deceive wise and eminent men, for one woman deceived Origin and another Paulo. . . . And in our day serious events have occurred which could be seen as confirmation of this truth, but I do not need to elaborate.   (p. 402)

His experience as the prosecutor in the outbreak of Illuminism in Extremadura had convinced him that trances were nothing more than erotic, diabolical possession:

[3] Enrique Llamas Martínez gives an account of the posthumous proceedings against Teresa's works and reproduces the relevant historical documents in *Santa Teresa de Jesús y la Inquisición española* (Madrid: Centro Superior de Investigaciones Científicas, 1972). All inter-textual page references are to this edition.

And when she says that in the fourth stage of prayer, one is lifeless and senseless, she is describing the effects of members of the [Illuminist] sect, who, possessed by Satan, are left lifeless and senseless and fall to the ground . . . ; we saw this many times in Extremadura . . . , especially among women, who when they are experiencing the supposed raptures are actually suffering from and being oppressed by the devil in the form of a succubus.   (pp. 411–412)

Fray Alonso was, in a modern sense, a very good reader of Teresa, alert to her ambiguities and rhetorical strategies. If we do not agree with his choice of the word "vanities," we must admit that he grasped the defensive function of her hyperbolic self-depreciation: "The author of this book writes a long history of her life and conversation and virtues, using the trivial excuse that she was ordered to do so by her confessors. Among the many words which have a humble sense, she says a million vanities" (p. 400). In his "close reading" of *The Way of Perfection* he rightly understood her implicit disdain for mechanical oral prayer. He notes that Teresa uses the word "prayer" with two meanings "in order to confuse her reader"; although she praises oral prayer, she really considers it "an entertaining preamble to that which she calls supernatural prayer" (p. 419). She mixes "oil with water"—sound doctrine with heresies (p. 398); she writes with "artifice and wiles," leaving the Catholic reader "unwary and deceived" (p. 419).

Fray Alonso was not alone in his opinion that Teresa's books should be banned. In 1598 the theologian Francisco de Pisa, though sympathetic to Teresa as a "virtuous woman," could not condone her encroachment on the male magisterial privilege:

In short, these books contain doctrine of an unlettered woman, who did not always heed the opinions of learned men and confessors, but acted according to her own thinking. . . . therefore, it seems that these books of Teresa should be gathered up, and not reprinted or translated into other languages, since there are many other books from which one can safely and profitably learn of the spiritual path, without having a woman come along and teach, for women are not given this office, but should wait in silence, as the apostle Saint Paul said.   (pp. 486–487)

One anonymous theologian, however, produced a surprising document in Teresa's defense. He not only defended the orthodox content of her writing but even suggested the possibility of a superior spiritual receptivity in women:

For even though the learned men (whom she consulted and obeyed) may know more about faith and Scripture and the general rules of prayer and contemplation, in the manner and means and particular experience of prayer, it may well be and often is that a woman knows more with the favor of God and with practice and experience than a speculative, dry, undevout theologian, and by dealing with a spiritual woman, to whom God gives great devotion, some of her devotion might stick to him, as Saint Thomas says . . . for learned men, confident in themselves and in their learning are guilty of pride and God is hidden from them, and women, lacking confidence in themselves, are humble and capable of being swelled with devotion for God: "thou hast hidden these things from the wise and understanding, and revealed them to babes: yea, Father, for such was thy gracious will (Matthew 11)."   (pp. 429–430)

Nonetheless, the same theologian who defended Teresa's works as theologically sound expressed his reservations about their dissemination: "But one could reasonably doubt whether it is wise for this book, which tells of visions, revelations, raptures and other very spiritual and delicate things, to circulate in the vernacular among the learned and the unlearned, religious and secular, men and women. For it may offer the occasion, especially for women, to be deceived, if they wanted to imitate the things that are written in it, or to feign them in order to deceive others" (p. 432). But, he concludes magnanimously, "if this book were the occasion for evil for some person, it would be his own fault, for there is nothing so good that the wicked cannot make ill use of it, as heretics have done with the Holy Scriptures . . ." (p. 433).

This, then, was the spectrum of theological opinions on Teresa's works in the decade following her death. For Fray Alonso Teresa was incapable of theological discourse; women's discourse was inherently unreliable; once seduced by the succubus of ecstasy, they inevitably were transformed into seducers. Pisa, while admitting to the *possibility* of orthodox feminine discourse, believed that the sex of the writer nevertheless rendered the content of such works superfluous. The anonymous theologian, like Báñez, was unable to cast aside the image of woman as easily seduced, but he chose Matthean over Pauline Scripture and conceded authority to feminine humility. By 1614 a few preachers were willing to suggest that God had been forced to use a woman as his agent on earth because of a shameful lack of worthy men.[4]

If Teresa's rhetoric was not unanimously successful with the theologians, it was successful enough. She had already won over a wider audience and was in the process of becoming the patron saint of the royal family. After years in Inquisitorial hands the manuscript of *The Book of Her Life* had found a safe haven in the library of Philip II at the Escorial.[5]

By the date of her beatification in 1614 Teresa's authority as a writer was not only accepted, it was sanctified: "How was it possible," wrote the Jesuit Cipriano de Aguayo,

[4] Félix G. Olmedo, "Santa Teresa de Jesús y los predicadores del siglo de oro," *Boletín de la Real Academia de la Historia* 84 (1924): 165–175 and 280–295 at 285.

[5] For the important role of the royal family in the beatification and canonization process see Francisco López Estrada, "Cohetes para Teresa: La relación de 1627 sobre las Fiestas de Madrid por el Patronato de España de Santa Teresa de Jesús y la polémica sobre el mismo," in *Congreso internacional Teresiano 4–7 octubre, 1982*, ed. Teófanes Egido Martínez et al. (Salamanca: Universidad de Salamanca, 1983), 2: 637–681.

"except by divine inspiration, for an ignorant woman to write what she did, and in such a particular style, plain and humble on the one hand, yet also grave and sententious, with such remarkable words, so pregnant with divine mysteries!"[6] Her acceptance as a miraculously inspired, charismatic writer is reflected in her earliest iconographic representations. The account of the celebrations in honor of her beatification describes four images of Teresa as writer. At this early date her identity as "Virgen y Doctora," symbolized by the palm branch and the golden pen, had already been established in the popular imagination.[7] According to Laura Gutiérrez Rueda, it is this image that appears most often in Teresian iconography. Ribera, Zubarán, Velázquez, and Alonso del Arco all portray Teresa with pen in hand. She frequently appears in ecstasy, as if attentive to a celestial voice who dictates what she is to write, while the dove of divine inspiration hovers over her head.[8]

In Counter-Reformation Spain Teresa's virtues—her verbal skill and personal persuasiveness—were so anomalous to her sex that they could only be considered miraculous. In a 1627 sermon in honor of Teresa's nomination as co-patron saint of Spain (an honor she was to share with Santiago de Compostela, the Moor Slayer), the Jesuit Rodrigo Niño declared: "Sanctity in women usually consists in being quiet, obeying, staying in a corner and forgetting

---

[6] Cited in Olmedo, "Santa Teresa de Jesús y los predicadores," p. 290. This idea is expressed repeatedly by witnesses for Teresa's beatification and canonization: her writing must be divinely inspired since it "surpasses the natural capacity of women" in style and content. For additional examples see Isaias Rodríguez, *Santa Teresa de Jesús y la espiritualidad española* (Madrid: Centro Superior de Investigaciones Científicas, 1972), pp. 80–81.

[7] Diego de San José, *Compendio de las solenes fiestas que en toda España se hicieron en la Beatificación de N. B. M. Teresa de Jesús Fundadora de la Reformación de Descalzos y Descalzas de N. S. de Carmen* (Madrid: Viuda de Alonso Martín, 1615).

[8] Gutiérrez Rueda, "Santa Teresa, escritora," in *Ensayo de iconografía teresiana*, número monográfico de *Revista de espiritualidad* 23 (1964): 61–78.

about oneself; O new miracle and rare prodigy! Not by keeping quiet, but by speaking, teaching and writing; not only by obeying, but by ordering, commanding, governing; not by observing enclosure but by traveling, disputing."[9] The only way to comprehend such virtue in a woman was to reassign her gender, to transform her into a "virile woman." Teresa was a prodigy because of her sex and a saint in spite of it. Her rhetoric of femininity, which served her own needs of self-assertion so successfully, also paradoxically sanctioned the paternalistic authority of the Church over its daughters and reinforced the ideology of women's intellectual and spiritual subordination. With her golden pen she won a public voice for herself, if not for other women.

[9] Quoted in López Estrada, "Cohetes para Teresa," p. 654.

BIBLIOGRAPHY

Editions of the Works of Teresa de Jesús

Camino de perfección. Transcripción del autógrafo de Valladolid. Edited by P. Tomás de la Cruz. 2 vols. Rome: Tipografia poliglotta vaticana, 1965.

Libro de la vida. Edited by Dámaso Chicharro. Madrid: Cátedra, 1979.

Obras completas. Edición manual. Edited by Efrén de la Madre de Dios and Otger Steggink. Madrid: Católica, 1962.

Obras completas. Nueva revisión del texto original con notas críticas. Edited by Efrén de la Madre de Dios, Otilio de Niño Jesús, and Otger Steggink. 3 vols. Madrid: Católica, 1951–1959.

Obras de Santa Teresa de Jesús. Edited by Silverio de Santa Teresa. Vols. 1–9 of Biblioteca mística carmelitana. Burgos: El Monte Carmelo, 1915–1924.

Translations

The Book of Her Life. Spiritual Testimonies. Soliloquies. Translated by Kieran Kavanaugh and Otilio Rodríguez. Vol. 1 of *The Collected Works of St. Teresa of Avila*. Washington, D.C.: Institute of Carmelite Studies, 1976.

The Complete Works of Saint Teresa of Jesus. Translated by E. Allison Peers. 3 vols. London: Sheed and Ward, 1944–1946.

The Interior Castle. Translated by Kieran Kavanaugh and Otilio Rodríguez. New York: Paulist Press, 1979.

The Letters of Saint Teresa of Jesus. Translated by E. Allison Peers. 2 vols. London: Burns, Oates and Washbourne, 1951.

List of Works Cited

Adnés, Pierre. "Mariage spirituel." In *Diccionnaire de spiritualité, ascétique et mystique*, edited by M. Viller et al., 10: 389–408. Paris: Beauchesne, 1977.

Alonso, Amado. "Noción, emoción, acción y fantasía en los diminutivos." In *Estudios lingüísticos: Temas españoles*, by Amado Alonso, pp. 193–299. Madrid: Gredos, 1951.

Alonso Cortés, Narciso. "Pleitos de los Cepedas." *Boletín de la Real Academia Española* 25 (1946): 85–110.

Alonso de Madrid. *Arte para servir a Dios*. 1521. Vol. 1 of *Místicos franciscanos*. Madrid: Católica, 1948.

Andrés, Melquíades. *La teología española en el siglo XVI*. 2 vols. Madrid: Católica, 1977.

Anglo, Sydney. "Melancholy and Witchcraft: The Debate between Wier, Bodin, and Scot." In *Folie et déraison à la Renaissance*, pp. 209–222. Brussels: Editions de la Université de Bruxelles, 1976.

Ardener, Edwin. "The 'Problem' Revisited." In *Perceiving Women*, edited by Shirley Ardener, pp. 19–27. New York: Wiley, 1975.

Ardener, Shirley, ed. *Perceiving Women*. New York: Wiley Press, 1975.

Aristotle. *The Nicomachean Ethics*. Translated by David Ross. London: Oxford University Press, 1925.

Babb, Lawrence. *The Elizabethan Malady: A Study of Melancholia in English Literature from 1580 to 1642*. East Lansing: Michigan State College Press, 1951.

Barrientos, Alberto, et al., eds. *Introducción a la lectura de Santa Teresa*. Madrid: Editorial de espiritualidad, 1978.

Bataillon, Marcel. *Erasmo y España*. Translated by Antonio Alatorre. 2d rev. ed. 1966. Reprint ed. Mexico: Fondo de cultura económica, 1982.

Bateson, Gregory, Don D. Jackson et al. "Toward a Theory of Schizophrenia." In *Steps to an Ecology of Mind* by Gregory Bateson, pp. 201–227. New York: Random House, 1972.

Beltrán de Heredia, Vicente. *Historia de la reforma de la provincia de España (1450–1550)*. Rome: Institutum Historicum FF. Praedicatorum, 1939.

Bernabéu Barrachina, Felicidad. "Aspectos vulgares del estilo teresiano y sus posibles razones." *Revista de espiritualidad* 22 (1963): 359–375.

Bilinkoff, Jodi. "The Social Meaning of Religious Reform: The Case of St. Teresa and Avila." *Archiv für Reformationsgeschichte* 79 (1988): 340–357.

Booth, Wayne. *A Rhetoric of Irony*. Chicago: University of Chicago Press, 1974.

Brouwer, Dédé. "The Influence of the Addressee's Sex on Politeness in Language Use." *Linguistics* 20 (1982): 697–711.

Brown, Penelope. "How and Why Are Women More Polite: Some Evidence from a Mayan Community." In *Women and Language in Literature and Society*, edited by Sally McConnell-Ginet, Ruth Borker, and Nelly Furman, pp. 111–136. New York: Praeger, 1980.

Brown, Penelope, and Stephen Levinson. "Social Structure, Group and Interaction." In *Social Markers in Speech*, edited by Klaus R. Scherer and Howard Giles, pp. 291–341. Cambridge: At the University Press, 1979.

―――. "Universals in Language Usage: Politeness Phenomena." In *Questions and Politeness: Strategies in Social Interaction*, edited by Esther Goody, pp. 56–289. Cambridge: At the University Press, 1978.

Bugge, John. *"Virginitas": An Essay in the History of a Medieval Ideal*. The Hague: Martinus-Nijhoff, 1975.

Bynum, Carolyn. *Holy Feast and Holy Fast: The Religious Significance of Food to Medieval Women*. Berkeley: University of California Press, 1987.

―――. *Jesus as Mother: Studies in the Spirituality of the High Middle Ages*. Berkeley: University of California Press, 1982.

Cameron, Deborah. *Feminism and Linguistic Theory*. London: Macmillan, 1985.

Caminero, Juventino. "Contexto sociocultural en el sistema místico de Santa Teresa." *Letras de Deusto* 14, no. 30 (1984): 27–48.

Carranza, Bartolomé. *Comentarios sobre el Catechismo christiano*. Edited by José I. Tellechea Idígoras. Madrid: Católica, 1972.

Carreño, Antonio. "Las paradojas del 'Yo' autobiográfico." In *Santa Teresa y la literatura mística hispánica*, edited by Manuel Criado de Val, pp. 255–64. Madrid: EDI–6, 1984.

Casares y Sánchez, Julio. *Diccionario ideológico de la lengua española*. 2d ed. Barcelona: Gustavo Gili, 1959.

Castro, Américo. *Teresa la Santa y otros ensayos*. Madrid: Alfaguara, 1972.

Censura de Carranza. Edited by José I. Tellechea Idígoras. Vol. 33 of *Archivo documental español*. Madrid: Real Academia de la Historia, 1981.

Cerdan, Francis. "Santa Teresa en *Los sermones del patronato* (1627)." In *Santa Teresa y la literatura mística hispánica*, edited by Manuel Criado de Val, pp. 601–608. Madrid: EDI–6, 1984.

Chorpenning, Joseph. "The Literary and Theological Method of *The Interior Castle.*" *Journal of Hispanic Philology* 3 (1979): 121–133.

———. "The Monastery, Paradise and the Castle: Literary Images and Spiritual Development in St. Teresa of Avila." *Bulletin of Hispanic Studies* 62 (1985): 245–257.

Christian, William A., Jr. *Apparitions in Late Medieval and Renaissance Spain.* Princeton, N.J.: Princeton University Press, 1981.

Cipar, Mary Cleopha. "The Portrait of Teresa of Avila as Woman and as Saint in *Camino de perfección.*" Ph.D. dissertation, University of Pittsburgh, 1983.

Colledge, Edmund, and James Walsh, eds. *Book of Showings* by Julian of Norwich. 2 vols. Toronto: Pontifical Institute of Mediaeval Studies, 1978.

Concha, Víctor García de la. *El arte literario de Santa Teresa.* Barcelona: Ariel, 1978.

———. "Exposición del *Cantar de los cantares.*" In *Academia literaria renascentista, vol. 1, Fray Luis de León,* edited by Víctor G. de la Concha, pp. 171–192. Salamanca: Ediciones Universidad de Salamanca, 1981.

Covarrubias, Sebastián de. *Tesoro de la lengua castellana o española.* 1611. Madrid: Turner, 1977.

Criado de Val, Manuel, ed. *Santa Teresa y la literatura mística hispánica.* Actas del I congreso internacional sobre Santa Teresa y la mística hispánica. Madrid: EDI–6, 1984.

Curtius, Ernst Robert. *European Literature and the Latin Middle Ages.* Translated by Willard R. Trask. 1953. Reprint ed. New York: Harper and Row, 1963.

De Ley, Margo. "The Prologue in Castilian Literature between 1200 and 1400." Ph.D. dissertation, University of Illinois, 1976.

Deneuville, Dominique. *Santa Teresa de Jesús y la mujer,* trans. Fernando Gutiérrez. Barcelona: Herder, 1966.

Diccionario de autoridades. 1726–1732. Edición facsímil. Madrid: Gredos, 1963.

Diego de San José. *Compendio de las solenes fiestas que en toda España se hicieron en la Beatificación de N. B. M. Teresa de Jesús Fundadora de la Reformación de Descalzos y Descalzas de N. S. de Carmen.* Madrid: Viuda de Alonso Martín, 1615.

Domínguez Ortiz, Antonio. *Los Judeoconversos en España y América.* Madrid: Istmo, 1971.

Efrén de la Madre de Dios and Otger Steggink. *Tiempo y vida de Santa Teresa*. 2d rev. ed. Madrid: Católica, 1977.

Egido, Aurora. "La configuración alegórica de *El castillo interior*." *Boletín del Museo e Instituto Camón Aznar* 10 (1983): 69–93.

———. "Los prólogos Teresianos y la 'santa ignorancia.' " In *Congreso internacional Teresiano 4–7 octubre, 1982*, edited by Teófanes Egido Martínez et al., 2: 581–607.

———. "Santa Teresa contra los letrados. Los interlocutores en su obra." *Criticón* 20 (1982): 85–121.

Egido Martínez, Teófanes, et al., eds. *Congreso internacional Teresiano 4–7 octubre, 1982*. 2 vols. Salamanca: Universidad de Salamanca, 1983.

Erasmus, Desiderius. *An Exhortation to the Diligent Study of Scripture*. 1529. Facsimile ed. Amsterdam: Theatrum Orbis Terrarum, 1973.

———. *La Paráclesis o exhortación al estudio de las letras divinas*. Edited by Dámaso Alonso. Madrid: Centro Superior de Investigaciones Científicas, 1971.

———. *Paraclesis ad lectorum pium*. In *Ausgewahlte Schriften*, edited by Werner Welzig. Vol. 3. Darmstadt: Wissenschaftliche Buchgesellschaft, 1968.

Fernández, Angel Raimundo. "Génesis y estructura de *Las moradas*." In *Congreso internacional Teresiano 4–7 octubre, 1982*, edited by Teófanes Egido Martínez et al., 2: 609–636. Salamanca: Universidad de Salamanca, 1983.

Flasche, Hans. "El problema de la certeza en el *Castillo interior*." In *Congreso internacional Teresiano 4–7 octubre, 1982*, edited by Teófanes Egido Martínez et al., 2: 447–458. Salamanca: Universidad de Salamanca, 1983.

Francisco de Osuna. *Tercer abecedario espiritual*. 1527. Edited by Melquíades Andrés. Madrid: Católica, 1972.

Fremaux-Crouzet, Annie. "L'antifeminisme comme theologie du pouvoir chez Melchor Cano." In *Hommage à Louise Bertrand (1921–1979): Etudes ibériques et latino-américaines*, pp. 139–186. Paris: Les Belles lettres, 1983.

Frenk, Margit. "'Lectores y oidores': La difusión oral de la literatura en el siglo de oro." In *Actas del séptimo congreso de la Asociación Internacional de Hispanistas*, edited by Giuseppe Bellini, 1: 101–123. Rome: Bulzone, 1982.

———. "Ver, oír, leer. . . ." In *Homenaje a Ana María Barrenechea*, edited by Lía Schwartz Lerner and Isaías Lerner, pp. 235–240. Madrid: Castalia, 1984.

Gerli, Michael. "El castillo interior y el Arte de la memoria." In Santa Teresa y la literatura mística hispánica, edited by Manuel Criado de Val, pp. 331–337. Madrid: EDI–6, 1984.

Giles, Howard, Richard Bourhis, and Donald Taylor. "Toward a Theory of Language in Ethnic Group Relations." In Language, Ethnicity and Intergroup Relations, edited by Howard Giles. European Monographs in Social Psychology, no. 13. London: Academic Press, 1977.

Giles, Howard, and Peter Powesland. Speech Style and Social Evaluation. European Monographs in Social Psychology, no. 7. London: Academic Press, 1975.

Giles, Howard, Klaus Scherer, and Donald Taylor. "Speech Markers in Social Interaction." In Social Markers in Speech, edited by Klaus R. Scherer and Howard Giles, pp. 343–381. Cambridge: At the University Press, 1979.

Gómez-Moriana, Antonio. "Autobiografía y discurso ritual: Problemática de la confesión autobiográfica destinada al tribunal inquisitorial." In Actes du IIe Colloque International de la Baume-les Aix, 23–24–25 mai 1981, pp. 69–94. Aix-en-Provence: Université de Provence, 1982. Reprinted in Imprévue 1 (1983): 107–129.

Gooch, Anthony. Diminutive, Augmentative and Pejorative Suffixes in Modern Spanish. 2d ed. Oxford: Pergamon, 1970.

Goody, Esther, ed. Questions and Politeness: Strategies in Social Interaction. Cambridge: At the University Press, 1978.

Gutiérrez Rueda, Laura. "Santa Teresa, escritora," in Ensayo de iconografía teresiana. Número monográfico de Revista de espiritualidad 23 (1964): 61–78.

Hatzfeld, Helmut. Estudios literarios sobre mística española. Madrid: Gredos, 1955.

———. Santa Teresa de Avila. New York: Twayne, 1968.

Hernadi, Paul. "Criticism as Re-presentation, Evaluation and Communication." In What is Criticism? edited by Paul Hernadi, pp. ix–xvi. Bloomington: Indiana University Press, 1981.

Hernando Balmori, Clemente. "Habla mujeril." Filología 8 (1962): 123–138.

Herrero, Javier. "The Knight and the Mystical Castle." Studies in Formative Spirituality 4 (1983): 393–407.

Hoornaert, Rodolphe. *Sainte Thérèse, écrivain, son milieu, ses facultés, son oeuvre*. Paris: Desclée de Brouwer, 1922.

Huerga, Alvaro. *Historia de los alumbrados (1570–1630)*. 3 vols. Madrid: Fundación universitaria española, 1978.

———. "Las lecturas místicas de los alumbrados." In *Santa Teresa y la literatura mística hispánica*, edited by Manuel Criado de Val, pp. 571–581. Madrid: EDI–6, 1984.

Imirizaldu, Jesús, ed. *Monjas y Beatas Embaucadoras*. Madrid: Editora Nacional, 1977.

Jerónimo Gracián de la Madre de Dios. *Obras*. Edited by Silverio de Santa Teresa. Vols. 15–17 of Biblioteca mística carmelitana. Burgos: El Monte Carmelo, 1933.

Kaufer, David. "Irony and Rhetorical Strategy." *Philosophy and Rhetoric* 10 (1977): 90–110.

———. "Irony and the Theory of Meaning." *Poetics Today* 4 (1983): 451–464.

Klaits, Joseph. *Servants of Satan: The Age of the Witch Hunts*. Bloomington: Indiana University Press, 1986.

Klibansky, Raymond, Erwin Panofsky, and Fritz Saxl. *Saturn and Melancholy: Studies in the History of Natural Philosophy, Religion, and Art*. London: Nelson, 1964.

Kramerae, Cheris. *Women and Men Speaking*. Rowley, Mass.: Newbury House, 1981.

———. "Women's Speech: Separate But Unequal?" In *Language and Sex: Difference and Dominance*, edited by Barrie Thorne and Nancy Henley, pp. 43–56. Rowley, Mass.: Newbury House, 1975.

Laguardia, Gari. "Santa Teresa and the Problem of Desire." *Hispania* 63 (1980): 523–530.

Lakoff, Robin. *Language and Women's Place*. New York: Harper and Row, 1975.

Lapesa, Rafael. *Historia de la lengua española*. 9th ed. Madrid: Gredos, 1984.

Lea, Charles Henry. *History of the Inquisition of Spain*. 1906–1907. 4 vols. Reprint ed. New York: American Scholar, 1966.

Lincoln, Victoria. *Teresa: A Woman. A Biography of Teresa de Avila*. Edited by Elias Rivers and Antonio de Nicolás. Albany: State University of New York Press, 1984.

Llamas-Martínez, Enrique. "El libro de la vida." In *Introducción a la lectura de Santa Teresa*, edited by Alberto Barrientos et al., pp. 210–219. Madrid: Editorial de espiritualidad, 1978.

Llamas-Martínez, Enrique. *Santa Teresa de Jesús y la Inquisición española*. Madrid: Centro Superior de Investigaciones Científicas, 1972.

———. "Teresa de Jesús y los alumbrados." In *Congreso internacional Teresiano 4–7 octubre, 1982*, edited by Teófanes Egido Martínez et al., 1: 137–167. Salamanca: Universidad de Salamanca, 1983.

Llorca, Bernardino. *La Inquisición española y los alumbrados (1509–1667)*. Salamanca: Universidad Pontíficia, 1980.

Longhurst, J. E. "La Beata Isabel de la Cruz ante la Inquisición, 1524–1529." *Cuadernos de historia de España* 25–26 (1957): 279–303.

López Estrada, Francisco. "Cohetes para Teresa: La relación de 1627 sobre las Fiestas de Madrid por el Patronato de España de Santa Teresa de Jesús y la polémica sobre el mismo." In *Congreso internacional Teresiano 4–7 octubre, 1982*, edited by Teófanes Egido Martínez et al., 2: 637–681. Salamanca: Universidad de Salamanca, 1983.

López Ibor, Juan José. "Ideas de Santa Teresa sobre la melancholía." *Revista de espiritualidad* 22 (1963): 423–443.

Luis de Granada. *Memorial de la vida cristiana*. 1565. In *Obras del V. P. M. Fray Luis de Granada*, edited by José Joaquín Mora. Vol. 2. Vol. 8 of Biblioteca de autores españoles. Madrid: Rivadeneyra, 1884.

McLaughlin, Eleanor Commo. "Equality of Souls, Inequality of Sexes: Women in Medieval Theology." In *Religion and Sexism*, edited by Rosemary Ruether, pp. 213–266. New York: Simon and Schuster, 1974.

Mandel, Adrienne Schizzano. "El 'Yo' narrador en el *Libro de su vida* de Santa Teresa." In *La Chispa '85': Selected Proceedings*, edited by Gilbert Paolini, pp. 231–242. New Orleans: Tulane, 1985.

Marco Merenciano, Francisco. *Ensayos médicos y literarios*. Madrid: Editorial Cultura hispánica, 1958.

Marichal, Juan. "Santa Teresa en el ensayismo hispánico." In *La voluntad de estilo*, by Juan Marichal, pp. 89–98. 1957. Reprinted ed. Madrid: Revista de Occidente, 1971.

Márquez, Antonio. *Los alumbrados: Orígenes y filosofía, 1525–1559*. 2d rev. ed. Madrid: Taurus, 1980.

———. *Literatura e Inquisición en España*. Madrid: Taurus, 1980.

Márquez Villaneuva, Francisco. "Santa Teresa y el linaje." In *Es-*

piritualidad y literatura en el siglo XVI, by Francisco Márquez Villaneuva, pp. 141–205. Madrid: Alfaguara, 1968.

———. "El símil del castillo interior: Sentido y génesis." In *Congreso internacional Teresiano 4–7 octubre, 1982*, edited by Teófanes Egido Martínez et al., 2: 495–522. Salamanca: Universidad de Salamanca, 1983.

———. "La vocación literaria de Santa Teresa." *Nueva revista de filología hispánica* 32 (1983): 355–374.

Martín del Blanco, Mauricio. *Santa Teresa de Jesús: Mujer de ayer para el hombre de hoy*. Bilbao: Mensajero, 1975.

Matos Schultz, Frances. "Autoridad e ideología en el *Libro de la vida* de Santa Teresa de Jesús." *Atenea* 2 (1982): 41–48.

Menéndez Pidal, Ramón. "El estilo de Santa Teresa." In *La lengua de Cristóbal Colón y otros estudios sobre el siglo XVI*, by Ramón Menéndez Pidal, pp. 119–142. 4th ed. Madrid: Espasa Calpe, 1958.

Midelfort, H. C. Erik. *Witch Hunting in Southwestern Germany, 1562–1682*. Stanford, Ca.: Stanford University Press, 1972.

Montes Giraldo, José Joaquín. "Funciones del diminutivo en español: Ensayo de clasificación." *Thesaurus* 27 (1972): 71–88.

Montgomery, Thomas, and Spurgeon Baldwin, eds. *El nuevo testamento según el manuscrito escurialense I–I–6*. Madrid: Anejos del Boletín de la Real Academia Española, 1970.

Morón Arroyo, Ciriaco. "'I Will Give You a Living Book': Spiritual Currents at Work at the Time of St. Teresa of Jesus." In *Centenary of St. Teresa*, edited by John Sullivan, pp. 95–112. Washington, D.C.: Institute of Carmelite Studies, 1984.

Náñez Fernández, Emilio. *El diminutivo: Historia y funciones en el español clásico y moderno*. Madrid: Gredos, 1973.

Nieto, J. C. "The Heretical Alumbrados Dexados: Isabel de la Cruz and Pedro Ruiz de Alcaraz." *Revue de littérature comparée* 52 (1978): 293–313.

Olmedo, Félix G. "Santa Teresa de Jesús y los predicadores del siglo de oro." *Boletín de la Real Academia de la Historia* 84 (1924): 165–175 and 280–295.

Olson, David. "Empirically Unbinding the Double Bind: Review of Research and Conceptual Reformulations." *Family Process* 11 (1972): 69–94.

Orozco Díaz, Emilio. *Expresión, comunicación y estilo en la obra de Santa Teresa*. Granada: Diputación provincial de Granada, 1987.

Ortega–Costa, Milagros, ed. *Proceso de la Inquisición contra María de Cazalla*. Madrid: Fundación universitaria española, 1978.

Pablo Maroto, Daniel de. "Camino de Perfección." In *Introducción a la lectura de Santa Teresa*, edited by Alberto Barrientos et al., pp. 269–310. Madrid: Editorial de espiritualidad, 1978.

————. *Dinámica de la oración: Acercamiento del orante moderno a Santa Teresa de Jesús*. Madrid: Editorial de espiritualidad, 1973.

Parvey, Constance F. "The Theology and Leadership of Women in the New Testament." In *Religion and Sexism*, edited by Rosemary Ruether, pp. 117–149. New York: Simon and Schuster, 1974.

Pedro de Rivadeneira, S. J. "Tratado de la tribulación." In *Obras escogidas*. Vol. 60 of Biblioteca de autores españoles. Madrid: Biblioteca de autores españoles, 1899.

Peers, Edgar Allison. "Saint Teresa's Style: A Tentative Appraisal." In *Saint Teresa of Jesus and Other Essays and Addresses*, pp. 81–135. London: Faber and Faber, 1953.

————. *Studies of the Spanish Mystics*. 1st ed. 3 vols. London: Sheldon, 1927.

————. *Studies of the Spanish Mystics*. 2d ed. London: Macmillan, 1951–.

Pérez, Joseph. "Cultura y sociedad en tiempos de Santa Teresa." In *Congreso internacional Teresiano 4–7 octubre, 1982*, edited by Teófanes Egido Martínez, 1: 31–40. Salamanca: Universidad de Salamanca, 1983.

Petroff, Elizabeth. *Medieval Women's Visionary Literature*. New York: Oxford, 1986.

Pope, Randolph. *La autobiografía española hasta Torres Villarroel*. Hispanistische Studien, Band 1. Frankfurt: Lang, 1974.

Porqueras Mayo, Alberto. *El prólogo en el Renacimiento español*. Madrid: Centro Superior de Investigaciones Científicas, 1965.

Proceso original que la Inquisición de Valladolid hizo al maestro Fr. Luis de Leon. Edited by Miguel Salvá and Pedro Sainz de Baranda. Vol. 10 of Colección de documentos inéditos para la historia de España. Madrid: Viuda de Calero, 1847.

Procesos de beatificación y canonización de Santa Teresa de Jesús. Edited by Silverio de Santa Teresa. Vols. 18–20 of Biblioteca mística carmelitana. Burgos: Tipografía de "El Monte Carmelo," 1934–1935.

Rey Tejerina, Arsenio. "Teresa de Jesús y su carnet de ortodoxia según su *Epistolario*." In *Santa Teresa y la literatura mística hispán*-

ica, edited by Manuel Criado de Val et al., pp. 109–115. Madrid: EDI–6, 1984.

Ricard, Robert. "Le symbolisme du *Chateau Intérieur* chez Sainte Thérèse." *Bulletin hispanique* 67 (1965): 25–41.

Rodríguez, Alfred, and Darcy Donahue. "Un ensayo de explicación razonada de las referencias de Santa Teresa a su propio sexo en *Vida*." In *Santa Teresa y la literatura mística hispánica*, edited by Manuel Criado de Val, pp. 309–313. Madrid: EDI–6, 1984.

Rodríguez, Isaias. *Santa Teresa de Jesús y la espiritualidad española*. Madrid: Centro Superior de Investigaciones Científicas, 1972.

Ruether, Rosemary. "The Persecution of Witches: A Case of Sexism and Agism." *Christianity and Crisis* 34 (1974): 291–295.

————, ed. *Religion and Sexism*. New York: Simon and Schuster, 1974.

Santa Teresa de Jesús, Doctora de la iglesia: Documentos oficiales del Proceso Canónico. Madrid: Editorial de espiritualidad, 1970.

Scherer, Klaus R., and Howard Giles, eds. *Social Markers in Speech*. Cambridge: At the University Press, 1979.

Selke, Angela. "El iluminismo de los conversos y la Inquisición. Cristianismo interior de los alumbrados: Resentimiento y sublimación." In *La Inquisición española: Nueva visión, nuevos horizontes*, edited by Joaquín Pérez Villaneuva, pp. 617–636. Madrid: Siglo veintiuno, 1980.

Serís, Homero. "Nueva genealogía de Santa Teresa." *Nueva revista de filología hispánica* 10 (1956): 365–384.

Slade, Carole. "Saint Teresa's *Meditaciones sobre los cantares*: The Hermeneutics of Humility and Enjoyment." *Religion and Literature* 18 (1986): 27–43.

Sluzki, Carlos, and Donald Ransom, eds. *Double Bind: The Foundation of the Communicational Approach to the Family*. New York: Grune and Strathon, 1976.

Smith, Paul Julian. "Writing Women in Golden Age Spain: Saint Teresa and María de Zayas." *MLN* 102 (1987): 220–240.

Smith, Philip M. "Sex Markers in Speech." In *Social Markers in Speech*, edited by Klaus R. Scherer and Howard Giles, pp. 109–146. Cambridge: At the University Press, 1979.

Sonnino, Lee A. *A Handbook to Sixteenth-Century Rhetoric*. New York: Barnes and Noble, 1968.

Sperber, Dan, and Deirdre Wilson. "Irony and the Use-Mention

Distinction." In *Radical Pragmatics*, edited by Peter Cole, pp. 295–318. New York: Academic Press, 1981.

Sullivan, Mary C. "From Narrative to Proclamation: A Rhetorical Analysis of the Autobiography of Teresa of Avila." *Thought* 58 (1983): 453–471.

Surtz, Ronald E. "La madre Juana de la Cruz (1481–1534) y la cuestión de la autoridad religiosa femenina." *Nueva revista de filología hispánica* 33 (1984): 483–491.

Swietlicki, Catherine. *Spanish Christian Cabala: The Works of Luis de León, Santa Teresa de Jesús, and San Juan de la Cruz.* Columbia: University of Missouri Press, 1986.

Szasz, Thomas. *The Myth of Mental Illness.* 1961. Reprint ed. New York: Harper and Row, 1974.

Thorne, Barrie. "Opening a Second Decade of Research." In *Language, Gender and Society*, edited by Barrie Thorne, Cheris Kramerae, and Nancy Henly, pp. 7–24. Newbury, Mass.: Rowley, 1983.

Trinidad, Francisco. "Lectura 'heterodoxa' de Santa Teresa." *Cuadernos del norte* 2 (1982): 2–8.

Veith, Ilza. *Hysteria: The History of a Disease.* Chicago: University of Chicago Press, 1965.

Villacèque, Sol. "Rhetorique et pragmatique: La transformation du code dans le *Libro de la vida* de Thérèse D'Avila." *Imprévue* 2 (1985): 7–27.

Weakland, John H. "The 'Double Bind' Hypothesis of Schizophrenia and Three-Party Interaction." In *Double Bind: The Foundation of the Communicational Approach to the Family*, edited by Carlos Sluzki and Donald Ransom, pp. 23–38. New York: Grune and Strathon, 1976.

Weber, Alison. "Teresa's 'Delicious' Diminutives: Pragmatics and Style in *Camino de perfección*." *Journal of Hispanic Philology* 10 (1986): 211–227.

Weinstein, Donald, and Rudolph Bell. *Saints and Society: The Two Worlds of Western Christendom, 1000–1700.* Chicago: University of Chicago Press, 1982.

Zuloaga Ospina, Alberto. "La función del diminutivo en español." *Thesaurus* 25 (1970): 23–48.

INDEX

accentuation, 13
Aguayo, Cipriano de, 163
Alcaraz, Pedro Ruiz de, 24n.15, 27
allegory, 98–99. See also *miles Christi* allegory; *sponsa Christi* allegory
Alonso de la Fuente, 121, 159–161, 163
Alonso de Madrid, 46
Alvarez, Baltasar, 43n.5, 67, 70
Anatomy of Melancholy, 140
aristocracy, Teresa's relations with, 4, 130–131
Aristotle, 15, 87, 139
arrobamiento (rapture), 40, 70–71, 121, 136, 137–139, 146
asceticism, Teresa's attitude toward, 140–143, 147–148
attenuation, 13
Augustine, Saint, 50, 51, 52
autobiography, as genre, 42–43

Báñez, Domingo, 43n.5, 47n.13, 77, 78, 117, 131; defense of Teresa, 158–159, 163
Bartolomé de Medina, 36
Bataillon, Marcel, 23, 28n.30
beatas, 4, 120–121
Beatriz de la Encarnación, 147
Beatriz de la Madre de Dios (Chávez), 150–156
Becedas, priest of, 57–59
Bernabéu, Felicidad, 9
Book of Foundations (*Libro de las fundaciones*): and Carmelite Reform, 123–128; humor in, 128–134; textual history, 135, 155. See also convent life, and obedience; melancholy

Book of Her Life (*Libro de la vida*): and Inquisition, 35, 43n.4, 131, 163; textual history, 43–44, 66–67. See also *concessio*; double bind theory; humility
Booth, Wayne, 86
Brown, Penelope, 12, 65
Burton, Robert, 140, 144n.18
Bynum, Caroline, 20

cabala, 109–110, 119n.27
Cameron, Deborah, 93
Cano, Melchor, 31–32, 34
Canticles. See Song of Songs
captatio benevolentiae, 49, 50, 64–71
Carmelite Reform, 83–84, 99–100, 124–126, 128–133
Carranza de Mendoza, Bartolomé, 29–32
Castro, Américo, 8–10
Cazalla, María de, 23, 28
censorship, 35, 50–51n.18, 78–79, 82, 117. See also Index of Prohibited Books
Cepeda, Alonso Sánchez de (Teresa's father), 8, 52, 54–57, 62–63, 123–124
Cerda, Luisa de la, 67
Chávez, Beatriz. See Beatriz de la Madre de Dios
Cicero, 51
Cisneros, Cardinal. See Ximénez de Cisneros
Communion (sacrament), 91, 136–137, 136n.10
Conceptions of Love of God. See Meditations on the Song of Songs
concessio (strategy of concession), 36–41, 51–56